APOLLO

— *A RETROSPECTIVE ANALYSIS* —

by
Roger D. Launius

NASA History Office
Code IQ
Office of External Relations
NASA Headquarters
Washington, DC 20546

MONOGRAPHS IN AEROSPACE HISTORY NUMBER 3
NASA SP-2004-4503
Reprinted July 2004

PREFACE

The program to land an American on the Moon and return safely to Earth in the 1960s has been called by some observers a defining event of the twentieth century. Pulitzer Prize-winning historian Arthur M. Schlesinger, Jr., even suggested that when Americans two centuries hence study the twentieth century, they will view the Apollo lunar landing as *the* critical event of the century. While that conclusion might be premature, there can be little doubt but that the flight of *Apollo 11* in particular and the overall Apollo program in general was a high point in humanity's quest to explore the universe beyond Earth.

Since the completion of Project Apollo more than twenty years ago there have been a plethora of books, studies, reports, and articles about its origin, execution, and meaning. At the time of the twenty-fifth anniversary of the first landing, it is appropriate to reflect on the effort and its place in U.S. and NASA history. This monograph has been written as a means to this end. It presents a short narrative account of Apollo from its origin through its assessment. That is followed by a mission by mission summary of the Apollo flights and concluded by a series of key documents relative to the program reproduced in facsimile. The intent of this monograph is to provide a basic history along with primary documents that may be useful to NASA personnel and others desiring information about Apollo.

The author would like to acknowledge the assistance of those individuals who aided in the preparation of this monograph. Lee D. Saegesser, William S. Skerrett, and Jennifer M. Hopkins were instrumental in obtaining documents and photographs used in this study; J.D. Hunley edited and critiqued the text; Patricia Shephard helped prepare the manuscript; the staffs of the NASA Headquarters Library and the Scientific and Technical Information Program provided assistance in locating materials; Ellwood Anaheim laid out the monograph; and the NASA Headquarters Printing and Graphics Office handled printing. Portions of the manuscript have been published in a different form in Roger D. Launius, *NASA: A History of the U.S. Civil Space Program* (1994), and *Space Flight: The First Thirty Years* (1991).

This is the third publication in a new series of special studies prepared by the NASA History Office. The MONOGRAPHS IN AEROSPACE HISTORY series is designed to provide a wide variety of studies relative to the history of aeronautics and space. This series' publications are intended to be tightly focused in terms of subject, relatively short in length, and reproduced in an inexpensive format to allow timely and broad dissemination to researchers in aerospace history. Suggestions for additional publications in the MONOGRAPHS IN AEROSPACE HISTORY series are welcome.

ROGER D. LAUNIUS
July 1994

Acknowledgments for the Reprinted Version

Special thanks go to a variety of people who helped make this publication possible. First, thanks to Nadine Andreassen in the NASA History Office for suggesting that we reprint this monograph for the 35th anniversary of *Apollo 11*. Also in our office, Jennifer Troxell assembled the necessary materials and oversaw this project. In the Headquarters Printing and Design Office, Shelley Kilmer updated the layout of this monograph and designed a new, very attractive cover, and Michelle Cheston carefully edited this publication. Jeffrey McLean and James Penny expertly handled the printing process. Steven Johnson capably oversaw the work of these Printing and Design professionals. Last and certainly not least, we still owe a special debt of gratitude to Roger D. Launius, the former NASA Chief Historian and the author of this continually useful and popular publication.

Stephen J. Garber
NASA History Office
July 2004

APOLLO: A RETROSPECTIVE ANALYSIS

APOLLO

A RETROSPECTIVE ANALYSIS

INTRODUCTION

On 25 May 1961 President John F. Kennedy announced to the nation a goal of sending an American safely to the Moon before the end of the decade. This decision involved much study and review prior to making it public, and tremendous expenditure and effort to make it a reality by 1969. Only the building of the Panama Canal rivaled the Apollo program's size as the largest non-military technological endeavor ever undertaken by the United States; only the Manhattan Project was comparable in a wartime setting. The human spaceflight imperative was a direct outgrowth of it; Projects Mercury (at least in its latter stages), Gemini, and Apollo were each designed to execute it. It was finally successfully accomplished on 20 July 1969, when *Apollo 11*'s astronaut Neil Armstrong left the Lunar Module and set foot on the surface of the Moon.

THE KENNEDY PERSPECTIVE ON SPACE

In 1960 John F. Kennedy, a Senator from Massachusetts between 1953 and 1960, ran for president as the Democratic candidate, with party wheelhorse Lyndon B. Johnson as his running mate. Using the slogan, "Let's get this country moving again," Kennedy charged the Republican Eisenhower Administration with doing nothing about the myriad social, economic, and international problems that festered in the 1950s. He was especially hard on Eisenhower's record in international relations, taking a Cold Warrior position on a supposed "missile gap" (which turned out not to be the case) wherein the United States lagged far behind the Soviet Union in ICBM technology. He also invoked the Cold War rhetoric opposing a communist effort to take over the world and used as his evidence the 1959 revolution in Cuba that brought leftist dictator Fidel Castro to power. The Republican candidate, Richard M. Nixon, who had been Eisenhower's Vice President tried to defend his mentor's record but when the results were in Kennedy was elected by a narrow margin of 118,550 out of more than 68 million popular votes cast.[1]

Kennedy as president had little direct interest in the U.S. space program. He was not a visionary enraptured with the romantic image of the last American frontier in space and consumed by the adventure of exploring the unknown. He *was*, on the other hand, a Cold Warrior with a keen sense of *Realpolitik* in foreign affairs, and worked hard to maintain balance of power and spheres of influence in American/Soviet relations. The Soviet Union's non-military accomplishments in space, therefore, forced Kennedy to respond and to serve notice that the U.S. was every bit as capable in the space arena as the Soviets. Of course, to prove this fact, Kennedy had to be willing to commit national resources to NASA and the civil space program. The Cold War realities of the time, therefore, served as the primary vehicle for an expansion of NASA's activities and for the definition of Project Apollo as the premier civil space effort of the nation. Even more significant, from Kennedy's perspective the Cold War necessitated the expansion of the military space program, especially the development of ICBMs and satellite reconnaissance systems.[2]

While Kennedy was preparing to take office, he appointed an ad hoc committee headed by Jerome B. Wiesner of the Massachusetts Institute of Technology to offer suggestions for American efforts in space. Wiesner, who later headed the President's Science Advisory Committee (PSAC) under Kennedy, concluded that the issue of "national prestige" was too great to allow the Soviet Union leadership in space efforts, and therefore the U.S. had to enter the field in a substantive way. "Space exploration and exploits," he wrote in a 12 January 1961 report to the president-elect, "have captured the imagination of the peoples of the world. During the next few years the prestige of the United States will in part be determined by the leadership we demonstrate in space activities." Wiesner also emphasized the importance of practical non-military applications of space technology—communications, mapping, and weather satellites among others—and the necessity of keeping up the effort to exploit space for national security through such technologies as ICBMs and reconnaissance satellites. He tended to deemphasize the human spaceflight initiative for very practical reasons. American launch vehicle technology, he argued, was not well developed and the potential of placing an astronaut in space before the Soviets was slim. He thought human spaceflight was a high-risk enterprise with a low chance of success. Human spaceflight was also less likely to yield valuable scientific results than, and the U.S., Wiesner thought, should play to its strength in space science where important results had already been achieved.[3]

Kennedy only accepted part of what Wiesner recommended. He was committed to conducting a more vigorous space program than had been Eisenhower, but he was more interested in human spaceflight than either his predecessor or his science advisor. This was partly because of the drama surrounding Project Mercury and the seven astronauts that NASA was training.[4] Wiesner had cautioned Kennedy about the hyperbole associated with human spaceflight. "Indeed, by having placed the highest national priority on the MERCURY program we have strengthened the popular belief that man in space is the most important aim for our non-military space effort," Wiesner wrote. "The manner in which this program has been publicized in our press has further crystallized such belief."[5] Kennedy, nevertheless, recognized the tremendous public support arising from this program and wanted to ensure that it reflected favorably upon his administration.

But it was a risky enterprise—what if the Soviets were first to send a human into space? what if an astronaut was killed and Mercury was a failure?—and the political animal in Kennedy wanted to minimize those risks. The earliest Kennedy pronouncements relative to civil space activity directly addressed these hazards. He offered to cooperate with the Soviet Union, still the only other nation involved in launching satellites, in the exploration of space. In his inaugural address in January 1961 Kennedy spoke directly to Soviet Premier Nikita Khrushchev and asked him to cooperate in exploring "the stars."[6] In his State of the Union address ten days later, he asked the Soviet Union "to join us in developing a weather prediction program, in a new communications satellite program, and in preparation for probing the distant planets of Mars and Venus, probes which may someday unlock the deepest secrets of the Universe." Kennedy also publicly called for the peaceful use of space, and the limitation of war in that new environment.[7]

In making these overtures Kennedy accomplished several important political ends. First, he appeared to the world as the statesman by seeking friendly cooperation rather than destructive competition with the Soviet Union, knowing full well that there was little likelihood that Khrushchev would accept his offer. Conversely, the Soviets would appear to be monopolizing space for their own personal, and presumably military, benefit. Second, he minimized the goodwill that the Soviet Union enjoyed because of its own success in space *vis-à-vis* the U.S. Finally, if the Soviet Union accepted his call for cooperation, it would tacitly be recognizing the equality of the U.S. in space activities, something that would also look very good on the world stage.[8]

THE SOVIET CHALLENGE RENEWED

Had the balance of power and prestige between the United States and the Soviet Union remained stable in the spring of 1961, it is quite possible that Kennedy would never have advanced his Moon program and the direction of American space efforts might have taken a radically different course. Kennedy seemed quite happy to allow NASA to execute Project Mercury at a deliberate pace, working toward the orbiting of an astronaut sometime in the middle of the decade, and to build on the satellite programs that were yielding excellent results both in terms of scientific knowledge and practical application. Jerome Wiesner reflected: "If Kennedy could have opted out of a big space program without hurting the country in his judgment, he would have."[9]

Firm evidence for Kennedy's essential unwillingness to commit to an aggressive space program came in March 1961 when the NASA Administrator, James E. Webb, submitted a request that greatly expanded his agency's fiscal year 1962 budget so as to permit a Moon landing before the end of the decade. While the Apollo lunar landing program had existed as a longterm goal of NASA during the Eisenhower administration, Webb proposed greatly expanding and accelerating it. Kennedy's budget director, David E. Bell, objected to this large increase and debated Webb on the merits of an accelerated lunar landing program. In the end the president was unwilling to obligate the nation to a much bigger and more costly space program. Instead, in good political fashion, he approved a modest increase in the NASA budget to allow for development of the big launch vehicles that would eventually be required to support a Moon landing.[10]

A slow and deliberate pace might have remained the standard for the U.S. civil space effort had not two important events happened that forced Kennedy to act. The Soviet Union's space effort counted coup on the United States one more time not long after the new president took office. On 12 April 1961 Soviet Cosmonaut Yuri Gagarin became the first human in space with a one-orbit mission aboard the spacecraft *Vostok 1*. The chance to place a human in space before the Soviets did so had now been lost. The great success of that feat made the gregarious Gagarin a global hero, and he was an effective spokesman for the Soviet Union until his death in 1967 from an unfortunate aircraft accident. It was only a salve on an open wound, therefore, when Alan Shepard became the first American in space during a 15-minute suborbital flight on 5 May 1961 by riding a Redstone booster in his *Freedom 7* Mercury spacecraft.[11]

Comparisons between the Soviet and American flights were inevitable afterwards. Gagarin had flown around the Earth; Shepard had been the cannonball shot from a gun. Gagarin's Vostok spacecraft had weighed 10,428 pounds; *Freedom 7* weighed 2,100 pounds. Gagarin had been weightless for 89 minutes; Shepard for only 5 minutes. "Even though the United States is still the strongest military power and leads in many aspects of the space race," wrote journalist Hanson Baldwin in the *New York Times* not long after Gagarin's flight, "the world—impressed by the spectacular Soviet firsts—believes we lag militarily and technologically."[12] By any unit of measure the U.S. had not demonstrated technical equality with the Soviet Union, and that fact worried national leaders because of what it would mean in the larger Cold War environment. These apparent disparities in technical competence had to be addressed, and Kennedy had to find a way to reestablish the nation's credibility as a technological leader before the world.

Close in the wake of the Gagarin achievement, the Kennedy Administration suffered another devastating blow in the Cold War that contributed to the sense that action had to be taken. Between 15 and 19 April 1961 the administration supported the abortive Bay of Pigs invasion of Cuba designed to overthrow Castro. Executed by anti-Castro Cuban refugees armed and trained by the CIA, the invasion was a debacle almost from the beginning. It was predicated on an assumption that the Cuban people would rise up to welcome the invaders and when that proved to be false, the attack could not succeed. American backing of the invasion was a great embarrassment both to Kennedy personally and to his administration. It damaged U.S. relations with foreign nations enormously, and made the communist world look all the more invincible.[13]

While the Bay of Pigs invasion was never mentioned explicitly as a reason for stepping up U.S. efforts in space, the international situation certainly played a role as Kennedy scrambled to recover a measure of national dignity. Wiesner reflected, "I don't think anyone can measure it, but I'm sure it [the invasion] had an impact. I think the President felt some pressure to get something else in the foreground."[14] T. Keith Glennan, NASA Administrator under Eisenhower, immediately linked the invasion and the Gagarin flight together as the seminal events leading to Kennedy's announcement of the Apollo decision. He confided in his diary that "In the aftermath of that [Bay of Pigs] fiasco, and because of the successful orbiting of astronauts by the Soviet Union, it is my opinion that Mr. Kennedy asked for a reevaluation of the nation's space program."[15]

REEVALUATING NASA'S PRIORITIES

Two days after the Gagarin flight on 12 April, Kennedy discussed once again the possibility of a lunar landing program with Webb, but the NASA head's conservative estimates of a cost of more than $20 billion for the project was too steep and Kennedy delayed making a decision. A week later, at the time of the Bay of Pigs invasion, Kennedy called Johnson, who headed the National Aeronautics and Space Council, to the White House to discuss strategy for catching up with the Soviets in space. Johnson agreed to take the matter up with the Space Council and to recommend a course of action. It is likely that one of the explicit programs that Kennedy asked Johnson to consider was a lunar landing program, for the next day, 20 April 1961, he followed up with a memorandum to Johnson raising fundamental questions about the project. In particular, Kennedy asked

> Do we have a chance of beating the Soviets by putting a laboratory in space, or by a trip around the moon, or by a rocket to go to the moon and back with a man? Is there any other space program that promises dramatic results in which we could win?[16]

While he waited for the results of Johnson's investigation, this memo made it clear that Kennedy had a pretty good idea of what he wanted to do in space. He confided in a press conference on 21 April that he was leaning toward committing the nation to a large-scale project to land Americans on the Moon. "If we can get to the moon before the Russians, then we should," he said, adding that he had asked his vice president to review options for the space program.[17] This was the first and last time that Kennedy said anything in public about a lunar landing program until he officially unveiled the plan. It is also clear that Kennedy approached the lunar landing effort essentially as a response to the competition between the U.S. and the U.S.S.R. For Kennedy the Moon landing program, conducted in the tense Cold War environment of the early 1960s, was a strategic decision directed toward advancing the far-flung interests of the United States in the international arena. It aimed toward recapturing the prestige that the nation had lost as a result of Soviet successes and U.S. failures. It was, as political scientist John M. Logsdon has suggested, "one of the last major political acts of the Cold War. The Moon Project was chosen to symbolize U.S. strength in the head-to-head global competition with the Soviet Union."[18]

Lyndon Johnson probably understood these circumstances very well, and for the next two weeks his Space Council diligently considered, among other possibilities, a lunar landing before the Soviets. As early as 22 April, NASA's Deputy Administrator Hugh L. Dryden had responded to a request for information from the National Aeronautics and Space Council about a Moon program by writing that there was "a chance for the U.S. to be the first to land a man on the moon and return him to earth if a determined national effort is made." He added that the earliest this feat could be accomplished was 1967, but that to do so would cost about $33 billion, a figure $10 billion more than the whole projected NASA budget for the next ten years.[19] A week later Wernher von Braun, director of NASA's George C. Marshall Space Flight Center at Huntsville, Alabama, and head of the big booster program needed for the lunar effort, responded to a similar request for information from Johnson. He told the vice president that "we have a sporting chance of sending a 3-man crew *around the moon* ahead of the Soviets" and "an excellent chance of beating the Soviets to the *first landing of a crew on the moon* (including return capability, of course.)" He added that "with an all-out crash program" the U.S. could achieve a landing by 1967 or 1968.[20]

After gaining these technical opinions, Johnson began to poll political leaders for their sense of the propriety of committing the nation to an accelerated space program with Project Apollo as its centerpiece. He brought in Senators Robert Kerr (D-OK) and Styles Bridges (R-NH) and spoke with several Representatives to ascertain if they were willing to support an accelerated space program. While only a few were hesitant, Robert Kerr worked to allay their concerns. He called on James Webb, who had worked for his business conglomerate during the 1950s, to give him a straight answer about the project's feasibility. Kerr told his congressional colleagues that Webb

was enthusiastic about the program and "that if Jim Webb says we can a land a man on the moon and bring him safely home, then it can be done." This endorsement secured considerable political support for the lunar project. Johnson also met with several businessmen and representatives from the aerospace industry and other government agencies to ascertain the consensus of support for a new space initiative. Most of them also expressed support.[21]

Air Force General Bernard A. Schriever, commander of the Air Force Systems Command that developed new technologies, expressed the sentiment of many people by suggesting that an accelerated lunar landing effort "would put a focus on our space program." He believed it was important for the U.S. to build international prestige and that the return was more than worth the price to be paid.[22] Secretary of State Dean Rusk, a member of the Space Council, was also a supporter of the initiative because of the Soviet Union's image in the world. He wrote to the Senate Space Committee a little later that "We must respond to their conditions; otherwise we risk a basic misunderstanding on the part of the uncommitted countries, the Soviet Union, and possibly our allies concerning the direction in which power is moving and where long-term advantage lies."[23] It was clear early in these deliberations that Johnson was in favor of an expanded space program in general and a maximum effort to land an astronaut on the Moon. Whenever he heard reservations Johnson used his forceful personality to persuade. "Now," he asked, "would you rather have us be a second-rate nation or should we spend a little money?"[24]

In an interim report to the president on 28 April 1961, Johnson concluded that "The U.S. can, if it will, firm up its objectives and employ its resources with a reasonable chance of attaining world leadership in space during this decade," and recommended committing the nation to a lunar landing.[25] In this exercise Johnson had built, as Kennedy had wanted, a strong justification for undertaking Project Apollo but he had also moved on to develop a greater consensus for the objective among key government and business leaders.

THE NASA POSITION

While NASA's leaders were generally pleased with the course Johnson was recommending—they recognized and mostly agreed with the political reasons for adopting a determined lunar landing program—they wanted to shape it as much as possible to the agency's particular priorities. NASA Administrator James Webb, well known as a skilled political operator who could seize an opportunity, organized a short-term effort to accelerate and expand a long-range NASA master plan for space exploration. A fundamental part of this effort addressed a legitimate concern that the scientific and technological advancements for which NASA had been created not be eclipsed by the political necessities of international rivalries. Webb conveyed the concern of the agency's technical and scientific community to Jerome Wiesner on 2 May 1961, noting that "the most careful consideration must be given to the scientific and technological components of the total program and how to present the picture to the world and to our own nation of a program that has real value and validity and from which solid additions to knowledge can be made, even if every one of the specific so-called 'spectacular' flights or events are done after they have been accomplished by the Russians." He asked that Wiesner help him "make sure that this component of solid, and yet imaginative, total scientific and technological value is built in."[26]

Partly in response to this concern, Johnson asked NASA to provide for him a set of specific recommendations on how a scientifically-viable Project Apollo, would be accomplished by the end of the decade. What emerged was a comprehensive space policy planning document that had the lunar landing as its centerpiece but that attached several ancillary funding items to enhance the program's scientific value and advance space exploration on a broad front:

1. Spacecraft and boosters for the human flight to the Moon.
2. Scientific satellite probes to survey the Moon.
3. A nuclear rocket.
4. Satellites for global communications.
5. Satellites for weather observation.
6. Scientific projects for Apollo landings.

Johnson accepted these recommendations and passed them to Kennedy who approved the overall plan.[27]

The last major area of concern was the timing for the Moon landing. The original NASA estimates had given a target date of 1967, but as the project became more crystallized agency leaders recommended not committing to such a strict deadline.[28] James Webb, realizing the problems associated with meeting target dates based on NASA's experience in space flight, suggested that the president commit to a landing by the end of the decade, giving the agency another two years to solve any problems that might arise. The White House accepted this proposal.[29]

DECISION

President Kennedy unveiled the commitment to execute Project Apollo on 25 May 1961 in a speech on "Urgent National Needs," billed as a second State of the Union message. He told Congress that the U.S. faced extraordinary challenges and needed to respond extraordinarily. In announcing the lunar landing commitment he said:

> If we are to win the battle that is going on around the world between freedom and tyranny, if we are to win the battle for men's minds, the dramatic achievements in space which occurred in recent weeks should have made clear to us all, as did the Sputnik in 1957, the impact of this adventure on the minds of men everywhere who are attempting to make a determination of which road they should take . . . We go into space because whatever mankind must undertake, free men must fully share.

Then he added: "I believe this Nation should commitment itself to achieving the goal, before this decade is out, of landing a man on the moon and returning him safely to earth. No single space project in this period will be more impressive to mankind, or more important for the long-range exploration of space; and none will be so difficult or expensive to accomplish."[30]

AN ASSESSMENT OF THE DECISION

The President had correctly gauged the mood of the nation. His commitment captured the American imagination and was met with overwhelming support. No one seemed concerned either about the difficulty or about the expense at the time. Congressional debate was perfunctory and NASA found itself literally pressing to expend the funds committed to it during the early 1960s. Like most political decisions, at least in the U.S. experience, the decision to carry out Project Apollo was an effort to deal with an unsatisfactory situation (world perception of Soviet leadership in space and technology). As such Apollo was a remedial action ministering to a variety of political and emotional needs floating in the ether of world opinion. Apollo addressed these problems very well, and was a worthwhile action if measured only in those terms. In announcing Project Apollo Kennedy put the world on notice that the U.S. would not take a back seat to its superpower rival. John Logsdon commented: "By entering the race with such a visible and dramatic commitment, the United States effectively undercut Soviet space spectaculars without doing much except

President John F. Kennedy addressing a joint session of Congress on 25 May 1961, on "Urgent National Needs." In this speech he announced the Apollo decision to land an American safely on the Moon before the end of the decade. NASA Photo #70-H-1075.

announcing its intention to join the contest."[31] It was an effective symbol, just as Kennedy had intended.

It also gave the U.S. an opportunity to shine. The lunar landing was so far beyond the capabilities of either the United States or the Soviet Union in 1961 that the early lead in space activities taken by the Soviets would not predetermine the outcome. It gave the U.S. a reasonable chance of overtaking the Soviet Union in space activities and recovering a measure of lost status.

Even though Kennedy's political objectives were essentially achieved with the decision to go to the Moon, there were other aspects of the Apollo commitment that require assessment. Those who wanted to see a vigorous space program, a group led by NASA scientists and engineers, obtained their wish with Kennedy's announcement. An opening was present to this group in 1961 that had not existed at any time during the Eisenhower Administration, and they made the

most of it. They inserted into the overall package supporting Apollo additional programs that they believed would greatly strengthen the scientific and technological return on the investment to go to the Moon. In addition to seeking international prestige, this group proposed an accelerated and integrated national space effort incorporating both scientific and commercial components.

In the end a unique confluence of political necessity, personal commitment and activism, scientific and technological ability, economic prosperity, and public mood made possible the 1961 decision to carry out a forward-looking lunar landing program. What perhaps should be suggested is that a complex web or system of ties between various people, institutions, and interests allowed the Apollo decision.[32] It then fell to NASA and other organizations of the Federal Government to accomplish the task set out in a few short paragraphs by President Kennedy.

GEARING UP FOR PROJECT APOLLO

The first challenge NASA leaders faced in meeting the presidential mandate was securing funding. While Congress enthusiastically appropriated funding for Apollo immediately after the president's announcement, NASA Administrator James E. Webb was rightly concerned that the momentary sense of crisis would subside and that the political consensus present for Apollo in 1961 would abate. He tried, albeit without much success, to lock the presidency and the Congress into a long-term obligation to support the program. While they had made an intellectual commitment, NASA's leadership was concerned that they might renege on the economic part of the bargain at some future date.[33]

Initial NASA estimates of the costs of Project Apollo were about $20 billion through the end of the decade, a figure approaching $150 billion in 1992 when accounting for inflation. Webb quickly stretched those initial estimates for Apollo as far as possible, with the intent that even if NASA did not receive its full budget requests, as it did not during the latter half of the decade, it would still be able to complete Apollo. At one point in 1963, for instance, Webb came forward with a NASA funding projection through 1970 for more than $35 billion. As it turned out Webb was able to sustain the momentum of Apollo through the decade, largely because of his rapport with key members of Congress and with Lyndon B. Johnson, who became president in November 1963.[34]

Project Apollo, backed by sufficient funding, was the tangible result of an early national commitment in response to a perceived threat to the United States by the Soviet Union. NASA leaders recognized that while the size of the task was enormous, it was still technologically and financially within their grasp, but they had to move forward quickly. Accordingly, the space agency's annual budget increased from $500 million in 1960 to a high point of $5.2 billion in 1965.[35] The NASA funding level represented 5.3 percent of the federal budget in 1965. A comparable percentage of the $1.23 trillion Federal budget in 1992 would have equaled more than $65 billion for NASA, whereas the agency's actual budget then stood at less than $15 billion.

Out of the budgets appropriated for NASA each year approximately 50 percent went directly for human spaceflight, and the vast majority of that went directly toward Apollo. Between 1959 and 1973 NASA spent more than $25 billion on human spaceflight, exclusive of infrastructure and support, of which nearly

$20 billion was for Apollo.[36] In addition, Webb sought to expand the definition of Project Apollo beyond just the mission of landing humans on the Moon. As a result even those projects not officially funded under the Apollo line item could be justified as supporting the mission, such as the Ranger, Lunar Orbiter, and Surveyor satellite probes.

For seven years after Kennedy's Apollo decision, through October 1968, James Webb politicked, coaxed, cajoled, and maneuvered for NASA in Washington. A longtime Washington insider—the former director of the Bureau of the Budget and Undersecretary of State during the Truman Administration—he was a master at bureaucratic politics, understanding that it was essentially a system of mutual give and take. For instance, while the native North Carolinian may also have genuinely believed in the Johnson Administration's Civil Rights bill that went before Congress in 1964, as a personal favor to the President he lobbied for its passage on Capitol Hill. This secured for him Johnson's gratitude, which he then use to secure the administration's backing of NASA's initiatives. In addition, Webb wielded the money appropriated for Apollo to build up a constituency for NASA that was both powerful and vocal. This type of gritty pragmatism also characterized Webb's dealings with other government officials and members of Congress throughout his tenure as administrator. When give and take did not work, as was the case on occasion with some members of Congress, Webb used the presidential directive as a hammer to get his way. Usually this proved successful. After Kennedy's assassination in 1963, moreover, he sometimes appealed for continued political support for Apollo because it represented a fitting tribute to the fallen leader. In the end, through a variety of methods Administrator Webb built a seamless web of political liaisons that brought continued support for and resources to accomplish the Apollo Moon landing on the schedule Kennedy had announced.[37]

Funding was not the only critical component for Project Apollo. To realize the goal of Apollo under the strict time constraints mandated by the president, personnel had to be mobilized. This took two forms. First, by 1966 the agency's civil service rolls had grown to 36,000 people from the 10,000 employed at NASA in 1960. Additionally, NASA's leaders made an early decision that they would have to rely upon outside researchers and technicians to complete Apollo, and contractor employees working on the program increased by a factor of 10, from 36,500 in 1960 to 376,700 in 1965. Private industry, research institutions, and universities, therefore, provided the majority of personnel working on Apollo.[38]

To incorporate the great amount of work undertaken for the project into the formal bureaucracy never seemed a particularly savvy idea, and as a result during the 1960s somewhere between 80 and 90 percent of NASA's overall budget went for contracts to purchase goods and services from others. Although the magnitude of the endeavor had been much smaller than with Apollo, this reliance on the private sector and universities for the bulk of the effort originated early in NASA's history under T. Keith Glennan, in part because of the Eisenhower Administration's mistrust of large government establishments. Although neither Glennan's successor, nor Kennedy shared that mistrust, they found that it was both good politics and the best way of getting Apollo done on the presidentially-approved schedule. It was also very nearly the only way to harness talent and institutional resources already in existence in the emerging aerospace industry and the country's leading research universities.[39]

In addition to these other resources, NASA moved quickly during the early 1960s to expand its physical capacity so that it could accomplish Apollo. In 1960 the space agency consisted of a small headquarters in Washington, its three inherited NACA research centers, the Jet Propulsion Laboratory, the Goddard Space Flight Center, and the Marshall Space Flight Center. With the advent of Apollo, these installations grew rapidly. In addition, NASA added three new facilities specifically to meet the demands of the lunar landing program. In 1962 it created the Manned Spacecraft Center (renamed the Lyndon B. Johnson Space Center in 1973), near Houston, Texas, to design the Apollo spacecraft and the launch platform for the lunar lander. This center also became the home of NASA's astronauts and the site of mission control. NASA then greatly expanded for Apollo the Launch Operations Center at Cape Canaveral on Florida's eastern seacoast. Renamed the John F. Kennedy Space Center on 29 November 1963, this installation's massive and expensive Launch Complex 39A was the site of the *Apollo 11* launch. Additionally, the spaceport's Vehicle Assemble Building was a huge and expensive 36-story structure where the Saturn/Apollo rockets were assembled. Finally, to support the development of the Saturn launch vehicle, in October 1961 NASA created on a deep south bayou the Mississippi Test Facility, renamed the John C. Stennis Space Center in 1988. The cost of this expansion was great, more than 2.2 billion over the decade, with 90 percent of it expended before 1966.[40]

THE PROGRAM MANAGEMENT CONCEPT

The mobilization of resources was not the only challenge facing those charged with meeting President Kennedy's goal. NASA had to meld disparate institutional cultures and approaches into an inclusive organization moving along a single unified path. Each NASA installation, university, contractor, and research facility had differing perspectives on how to go about the task of accomplishing Apollo.[41] To bring a semblance of order to the program, NASA expanded the "program management" concept borrowed by T. Keith Glennan in the late 1950s from the military/industrial complex, bringing in military managers to oversee Apollo. The central figure in this process was U.S. Air Force Major General Samuel C. Phillips, the architect of the *Minuteman* ICBM program before coming to NASA in 1962. Answering directly to the Office of Manned Space Flight at NASA headquarters, which in turn reported to the NASA administrator, Phillips created an omnipotent program office with centralized authority over design, engineering, procurement, testing, construction, manufacturing, spare parts, logistics, training, and operations.[42]

One of the fundamental tenets of the program management concept was that three critical factors—cost, schedule, and reliability—were interrelated and had to be managed as a group. Many also recognized these factors' constancy; if program managers held cost to a specific level, then one of the other two factors, or both of them to a somewhat lesser degree, would be adversely affected. This held true for the Apollo program. The schedule, dictated by the president, was firm. Since humans were involved in the flights, and since the president had directed that the lunar landing be conducted safely, the program managers placed a heavy emphasis on reliability. Accordingly, Apollo used redundant systems extensively so that failures would be both predictable and minor in result. The significance of both of these factors forced the third factor, cost, much higher than might have been the case with a more leisurely lunar program such as had been conceptualized in the latter 1950s. As it was, this was the price paid for success under the Kennedy mandate and program managers made conscious decisions based on a knowledge of these factors.[43]

The program management concept was recognized as a critical component of Project Apollo's success in November 1968, when *Science* magazine, the publication of the American Association for the Advancement of Science, observed:

In terms of numbers of dollars or of men, NASA has not been our largest national undertaking, but in terms of complexity, rate of growth, and technological sophistication it has been unique. . . It may turn out that [the space program's] most valuable spin-off of all will be human rather than technological: better knowledge of how to plan, coordinate, and monitor the multitudinous and varied activities of the organizations required to accomplish great social undertakings.[44]

Understanding the management of complex structures for the successful completion of a multifarious task was an important outgrowth of the Apollo effort.

This management concept under Phillips orchestrated more than 500 contractors working on both large and small aspects of Apollo. For example, the prime contracts awarded to industry for the principal components of just the Saturn V included the Boeing Company for the S-IC, first stage; North American Aviation—S-II, second stage; the Douglas Aircraft Corporation—S-IVB, third stage; the Rocketdyne Division of North American Aviation—J-2 and F-1 engines; and International Business Machines (IBM)—Saturn instruments. These prime contractors, with more than 250 subcontractors, provided millions of parts and components for use in the Saturn launch vehicle, all meeting exacting specifications for performance and reliability. The total cost expended on development of the Saturn launch vehicle was massive, amounting to $9.3 billion. So huge was the overall Apollo endeavor that NASA's procurement actions rose from roughly 44,000 in 1960 to almost 300,000 by 1965.[45]

Getting all of the personnel elements to work together challenged the program managers, regardless of whether or not they were civil service, industry, or university personnel. There were various communities within NASA that differed over priorities and competed for resources. The two most identifiable groups were the engineers and the scientists. As ideal types, engineers usually worked in teams to build hardware that could carry out the missions necessary to a successful Moon landing by the end of the decade. Their primary goal involved building vehicles that would function reliably within the fiscal resources allocated to Apollo. Again as ideal types, space scientists engaged in pure research and were more concerned with designing experiments that would expand scientific knowledge about the Moon. They also tended to be individualists, unaccustomed to regimentation and unwilling to concede gladly the direction of projects to outside entities. The two groups contended with each other over a great

variety of issues associated with Apollo. For instance, the scientists disliked having to configure payloads so that they could meet time, money, or launch vehicle constraints. The engineers, likewise, resented changes to scientific packages added after project definition because these threw their hardware efforts out of kilter. Both had valid complaints and had to maintain an uneasy cooperation to accomplish Project Apollo.

The scientific and engineering communities within NASA, additionally, were not monolithic, and differences among them thrived. Add to these groups representatives from industry, universities, and research facilities, and competition on all levels to further their own scientific and technical areas was the result. The NASA leadership generally viewed this pluralism as a positive force within the space program, for it ensured that all sides aired their views and emphasized the honing of positions to a fine edge. Competition, most people concluded, made for a more precise and viable space exploration effort. There were winners and losers in this strife, however, and sometimes ill-will was harbored for years. Moreover, if the conflict became too great and spilled into areas where it was misunderstood, it could be devastating to the conduct of the lunar program. The head of the Apollo program worked hard to keep these factors balanced and to promote order so that NASA could accomplish the presidential directive.[46]

Another important management issue arose from the agency's inherited culture of in-house research. Because of the magnitude of Project Apollo, and its time schedule, most of the nitty-gritty work had to be done outside NASA by means of contracts. As a result, with a few important exceptions, NASA scientists and engineers did not build flight hardware, or even operate missions. Rather, they planned the program, prepared guidelines for execution, competed contracts, and oversaw work accomplished elsewhere. This grated on those NASA personnel oriented toward research, and prompted disagreements over how to carry out the lunar landing goal. Of course, they had reason for complaint beyond the simplistic argument of wanting to be "dirty-handed" engineers; they had to have enough in-house expertise to ensure program accomplishment. If scientists or engineers did not have a professional competence on a par with the individuals actually doing the work, how could they oversee contractors actually creating the hardware and performing the experiments necessary to meet the rigors of the mission?[47]

One anecdote illustrates this point. The Saturn second stage was built by North American Aviation at its plant at Seal Beach, California, shipped to NASA's

Marshall Space Flight Center, Huntsville, Alabama, and there tested to ensure that it met contract specifications. Problems developed on this piece of the Saturn effort and Wernher von Braun began intensive investigations. Essentially his engineers completely disassembled and examined every part of every stage delivered by North American to ensure no defects. This was an enormously expensive and time-consuming process, grinding the stage's production schedule almost to a standstill and jeopardizing the Presidential timetable.

When this happened Webb told von Braun to desist, adding that "We've got to trust American industry." The issue came to a showdown at a meeting where the Marshall rocket team was asked to explain its extreme measures. While doing so, one of the engineers produced a rag and told Webb that "this is what we find in this stuff." The contractors, the Marshall engineers believed, required extensive oversight to ensure they produced the highest quality work. A compromise emerged that was called the 10 percent rule: 10 percent of all funding for NASA was to be spent to ensure in-house expertise and in the process check contractor reliability.[48]

HOW DO WE GO TO THE MOON?

One of the critical early management decisions made by NASA was the method of going to the Moon. No controversy in Project Apollo more significantly caught up the tenor of competing constituencies in NASA than this one. There were three basic approaches that were advanced to accomplish the lunar mission:

1. *Direct Ascent* called for the construction of a huge booster that launched a spacecraft, sent it on a course directly to the Moon, landed a large vehicle, and sent some part of it back to Earth. The Nova booster project, which was to have been capable of generating up to 40 million pounds of thrust, would have been able to accomplish this feat. Even if other factors had not impaired the possibility of direct ascent, the huge cost and technological sophistication of the Nova rocket quickly ruled out the option and resulted in cancellation of the project early in the 1960s despite the conceptual simplicity of the direct ascent method. The method had few advocates when serious planning for Apollo began.

2. *Earth-Orbit Rendezvous* was the logical first alternative to the direct ascent approach. It called for the launching of various modules required for the Moon trip into an orbit above the Earth, where they would rendezvous, be assembled into a single system, refueled, and sent to the Moon. This could be accomplished using the Saturn launch vehicle already under development by NASA and capable of generating 7.5 million pounds of thrust. A logical component of this approach was also the establishment of a space station in Earth orbit to serve as the lunar mission's rendezvous, assembly, and refueling point. In part because of this prospect, a space station emerged as part of the long-term planning of NASA as a jumping-off place for the exploration of space. This method of reaching the Moon, however, was also fraught with challenges, notably finding methods of maneuvering and rendezvousing in space, assembling components in a weightless environment, and safely refueling spacecraft.

3. *Lunar-Orbit Rendezvous* proposed sending the entire lunar spacecraft up in one launch. It would head to the Moon, enter into orbit, and dispatch a small lander to the lunar surface. It was the simplest of the three methods, both in terms of development and operational costs, but it was risky. Since rendezvous was taking place in lunar, instead of Earth, orbit there was no room for error or the crew could not get home. Moreover, some of the trickiest course corrections and maneuvers had to be done after the spacecraft had been committed to a circumlunar flight. The Earth-orbit rendezvous approach kept all the options for the mission open longer than the lunar-orbit rendezvous mode.[49]

Inside NASA, advocates of the various approaches contended over the method of flying to the Moon while the all-important clock that Kennedy had started continued to tick. It was critical that a decision not be delayed, because the mode of flight in part dictated the spacecraft developed. While NASA engineers could proceed with building a launch vehicle, the Saturn, and define the basic components of the spacecraft—a habitable crew compartment, a baggage car of some type, and a jettisonable service module containing propulsion and other expendable systems—they could not proceed much beyond rudimentary conceptions without a mode decision. The NASA Rendezvous Panel at Langley Research Center, headed by John C. Houbolt, pressed hard for the lunar-orbit rendezvous as the most expeditious means of accomplishing the mission. Using sophisticated technical and economic arguments, over a period of months in 1961 and 1962 Houbolt's group advocated and persuaded the rest of NASA's leadership that lunar-orbit rendezvous was not the risky proposition that it had earlier seemed.[50]

The last to give in was Wernher von Braun and his associates at the Marshall Space Flight Center. This group favored the Earth-orbit rendezvous because the direct ascent approach was technologically unfeasible before the end of the 1960s, because it provided a logical rationale for a space station, and because it ensured an extension of the Marshall workload (something that was always important to center directors competing inside the agency for personnel and other resources). At an all-day meeting on 7 June 1962 at Marshall, NASA leaders met to hash out these differences, with the debate getting heated at times. After more than six hours of discussion von Braun finally gave in to the lunar-orbit rendezvous mode, saying that its advocates had demonstrated adequately its feasibility and that any further contention would jeopardize the president's timetable.[51]

With internal dissention quieted, NASA moved to announce the Moon landing mode to the public in the summer of 1962. As it prepared to do so, however, Kennedy's Science Adviser, Jerome B. Wiesner, raised objections because of the inherent risk it brought to the crew. As a result of this opposition, Webb back-pedaled and stated that the decision was tentative and that NASA would sponsor further studies. The issue reached a climax at the Marshall Space Flight Center in September 1962 when President Kennedy, Wiesner, Webb, and several other Washington figures visited von Braun. As the entourage viewed a mock-up of a Saturn V first stage booster during a photo opportunity for the media, Kennedy nonchalantly mentioned to von Braun, "I understand you and Jerry disagree about the right way to go to the moon." Von Braun acknowledged this disagreement, but when Wiesner began to explain his concern Webb, who had been quiet until this point, began to argue with him "for being on the wrong side of the issue." While the mode decision had been an uninteresting technical issue before, it then

President John F. Kennedy visited Marshall Space Flight Center on 11 September 1962. Here President Kennedy and Dr. Wernher von Braun, MSFC Director, tour one of the laboratories. NASA MSFC Photo #9801807.

became a political concern hashed over in the press for days thereafter. The science advisor to British Prime Minister Harold Macmillan, who had accompanied Wiesner on the trip, later asked Kennedy on Air Force One how the debate would turn out. The president told him that Wiesner would lose, "Webb's got all the money, and Jerry's only got me."[52] Kennedy was right, Webb lined up political support in Washington for the lunar-orbit rendezvous mode and announced it as a final decision on 7 November 1962.[53] This set the stage for the operational aspects of Apollo.

PRELUDE TO APOLLO: MERCURY

At the time of the announcement of Project Apollo by President Kennedy in May 1961 NASA was still consumed with the task of placing an American in orbit through Project Mercury. Stubborn problems arose, however, at seemingly every turn. The first space flight of an astronaut, made by Alan B. Shepard, had been postponed for weeks so NASA engineers could resolve numerous details and only took place on 5 May 1961, less than three weeks before the Apollo announcement. The second flight, a suborbital mission like Shepard's, launched on 21 July 1961, also had problems. The hatch blew off prematurely from the Mercury capsule, *Liberty Bell 7,* and it sank into the Atlantic Ocean before it could be recovered. In the process the astronaut, "Gus" Grissom, nearly drowned before being hoisted to safety in a helicopter. These suborbital flights, however, proved valuable for NASA technicians who found ways to solve or work around literally thousands of obstacles to successful space flight.[54]

As these issues were being resolved, NASA engineers began final preparations for the orbital aspects of Project Mercury. In this phase NASA planned to use a Mercury capsule capable of supporting a human in space for not just minutes, but eventually for as much as three days. As a launch vehicle for this Mercury capsule, NASA used the more powerful Atlas instead of the Redstone. But this decision was not without controversy. There were technical difficulties to be overcome in mating it to the Mercury capsule to be sure, but the biggest complication was a debate among NASA engineers over its propriety for human spaceflight.[55]

When first conceived in the 1950s many believed Atlas was a high-risk proposition because to reduce its weight Convair Corp. engineers under the direction of Karel J. Bossart, a pre-World War II immigrant from Belgium, designed the booster with a very thin, internally pressurized fuselage instead of massive struts and a thick metal skin. The "steel balloon," as it was sometimes called, employed engineering techniques that ran counter to a conservative engineering approach used by Wernher von Braun for the V-2 and the Redstone at Huntsville, Alabama.[56] Von Braun, according to Bossart, needlessly designed his boosters like "bridges," to withstand any possible shock. For his part, von Braun thought the Atlas too flimsy to hold up during launch. He considered Bossart's approach much too dangerous for human spaceflight, remarking that the astronaut using the "contraption," as he called the Atlas booster, "should be getting a medal just for sitting on top of it before he takes off!"[57] The reservations began to melt away, however, when Bossart's team pressurized one of the boosters and dared one of von Braun's engineers to knock a hole in it with a sledge hammer. The blow left the booster unharmed, but the recoil from the hammer nearly clubbed the engineer.[58]

Most of the differences had been resolved by the first successful orbital flight of an unoccupied Mercury-Atlas combination in September 1961. On 29 November the final test flight took place, this time with the chimpanzee Enos occupying the capsule for a two-orbit ride before being successfully recovered in an ocean landing. Not until 20 February 1962, however, could NASA get ready for an orbital flight with an astronaut. On that date John Glenn became the first American to circle the Earth, making three orbits in his *Friendship 7* Mercury spacecraft. The flight was not without problems, however; Glenn flew parts of the last two orbits manually because of an autopilot failure and left his normally jettisoned retrorocket pack attached to his capsule during reentry because of a loose heat shield.

Glenn's flight provided a healthy increase in national pride, making up for at least some of the earlier Soviet successes. The public, more than celebrating the technological success, embraced Glenn as a personification of heroism and dignity. Hundreds of requests for personal appearances by Glenn poured into NASA headquarters, and NASA learned much about the power of the astronauts to sway public opinion. The NASA leadership made Glenn available to speak at some events, but more often substituted other astronauts and declined many other invitations. Among other engagements, Glenn did address a joint session of Congress and participated in several ticker-tape parades around the country. NASA discovered in the process of this hoopla a powerful public relations tool that it has employed ever since.[59]

Three more successful Mercury flights took place during 1962 and 1963. Scott Carpenter made three orbits on 20 May 1962, and on 3 October 1962 Walter Schirra flew six orbits. The capstone of Project Mercury was the 15-16 May 1963 flight of Gordon Cooper, who circled the Earth 22 times in 34 hours. The program had succeeded in accomplishing its purpose: to successfully orbit a human in space, explore aspects of tracking and control, and to learn about microgravity and other biomedical issues associated with spaceflight.[60]

BRIDGING THE TECHNOLOGICAL GAP: FROM GEMINI TO APOLLO

Even as the Mercury program was underway and work took place developing Apollo hardware, NASA program managers perceived a huge gap in the capability for human spaceflight between that acquired with Mercury and what would be required for a Lunar landing. They closed most of the gap by experimenting and training on the ground, but some issues required experience in space. Three major areas immediately arose where this was the case. The first was the ability in space to locate, maneuver toward, and rendezvous and dock with another spacecraft. The second was closely related, the ability of astronauts to work outside a spacecraft. The third involved the collection of more sophisticated physiological data about the human response to extended spaceflight.[61]

To gain experience in these areas before Apollo could be readied for flight, NASA devised Project Gemini. Hatched in the fall of 1961 by engineers at Robert Gilruth's Space Task Group in cooperation with McDonnell Aircraft Corp. technicians, builders of the Mercury spacecraft, Gemini started as a larger Mercury Mark II capsule but soon became a totally different proposition. It could accommodate two astronauts for extended flights of more than two weeks. It pioneered the use of fuel cells instead of batteries to power the ship, and incorporated a series of modifications to hardware. Its designers also toyed with the possibility of using a paraglider being developed at Langley Research Center for "dry" landings instead of a "splashdown" in water and recovery by the Navy. The whole system was to be powered by the newly developed *Titan II* launch vehicle, another ballistic missile developed for the Air Force. A central reason for this program was to perfect techniques for rendezvous and docking, so NASA appropriated from the military some Agena rocket upper stages and fitted them with docking adapters.

Problems with the Gemini program abounded from the start. The *Titan II* had longitudinal oscilla-

tions, called the "pogo" effect because it resembled the behavior of a child on a pogo stick. Overcoming this problem required engineering imagination and long hours of overtime to stabilize fuel flow and maintain vehicle control. The fuel cells leaked and had to be redesigned, and the Agena reconfiguration also suffered costly delays. NASA engineers never did get the paraglider to work properly and eventually dropped it from the program in favor of a parachute system the one used for Mercury. All of these difficulties shot an estimated $350 million program to over $1 billion. The overruns were successfully justified by the space agency, however, as necessities to meet the Apollo landing commitment.[62]

By the end of 1963 most of the difficulties with Gemini had been resolved, albeit at great expense, and the program was ready for flight. Following two unoccupied orbital test flights, the first operational mission took place on 23 March 1965. Mercury astronaut Grissom commanded the mission, with John W. Young, a Naval aviator chosen as an astronaut in 1962, accompanying him. The next mission, flown in June 1965 stayed aloft for four days and astronaut Edward H. White II performed the first extra-vehicular activity (EVA) or spacewalk.[63] Eight more missions followed through November 1966. Despite problems great and small encountered on virtually all of them, the program achieved its goals. Additionally, as a technological learning program Gemini had been a success, with 52 different experiments performed on the ten missions. The bank of data acquired from Gemini helped to bridge the gap between Mercury and what would be required to complete Apollo within the time constraints directed by the president.[64]

SATELLITE SUPPORT OF APOLLO

In addition to the necessity of acquiring the skills necessary to maneuver in space prior to executing the Apollo mandate, NASA had to learn much more about the Moon itself to ensure that its astronauts would survive. They needed to know the composition and geography of Moon, and the nature of the lunar surface. Was it solid enough to support a lander, was it composed of dust that would swallow up the spacecraft? Would communications systems work on the Moon? Would other factors—geology, geography, radiation, etc.—affect the astronauts? To answer these questions three distinct satellite research programs emerged to study the Moon. The first of these was Project Ranger, which had actually been started in the 1950s, in response to Soviet lunar exploration, but had been a notable failure until the mid-1960s when three probes photographed the lunar surface before crashing into it.[65]

The second project was the Lunar Orbiter, an effort approved in 1960 to place probes in orbit around the Moon. This project, originally not intended to support Apollo, was reconfigured in 1962 and 1963 to further the Kennedy mandate more specifically by mapping the surface. In addition to a powerful camera that could send photographs to Earth tracking stations, it carried three scientific experiments—selnodesy (the lunar equivalent of geodesy), meteoroid detection, and radiation measurement. While the returns from these instruments interested scientists in and of themselves, they were critical to Apollo. NASA launched five Lunar Orbiter satellites between 10 August 1966 and 1 August 1967, all successfully achieving their objectives. At the completion of the third mission, moreover, the Apollo planners announced that they had sufficient data to press on with an astronaut landing, and were able to use the last two missions for other activities.[66]

Finally, in 1961 NASA created Project Surveyor to soft-land a satellite on the Moon. A small craft with tripod landing legs, it could take post-landing photographs and perform a variety of other measurements. *Surveyor 1* landed on the Moon on 2 June 1966 and transmitted more than 10,000 high-quality photographs of the surface. Although the second mission crash landed, the next flight provided photographs, measurements of the composition and surface-bearing strength of the lunar crust, and readings on the thermal and radar reflectivity of the soil. Although *Surveyor 4* failed, by the time of the program's completion in 1968 the remaining three missions had yielded significant scientific data both for Apollo and for the broader lunar science community.[67]

BUILDING SATURN

NASA inherited the effort to develop the Saturn family of boosters used to launch Apollo to the Moon in 1960 when it acquired the Army Ballistic Missile Agency under Wernher von Braun.[68] By that time von Braun's engineers were hard at work on the first generation Saturn launch vehicle, a cluster of eight Redstone boosters around a Jupiter fuel tank. Fueled by a combination of liquid oxygen (LOX) and RP-1 (a version of kerosene), the *Saturn I* could generate a thrust of 205,000 pounds. This group also worked on a second stage, known in its own right as the Centaur, that used a revolutionary fuel mixture of LOX and

liquid hydrogen that could generate a greater ratio of thrust to weight. The fuel choice made this second stage a difficult development effort, because the mixture was highly volatile and could not be readily handled. But the stage could produce an additional 90,000 pounds of thrust. The *Saturn I* was solely a research and development vehicle that would lead toward the accomplishment of Apollo, making ten flights between October 1961 and July 1965. The first four flights tested the first stage, but beginning with the fifth launch the second stage was active and these missions were used to place scientific payloads and Apollo test capsules into orbit.[69]

The next step in Saturn development came with the maturation of the *Saturn IB*, an upgraded version of earlier vehicle. With more powerful engines generating 1.6 million pounds of thrust from the first stage, the two-stage combination could place 62,000-pound payloads into Earth orbit. The first flight on 26 February 1966 tested the capability of the booster and the Apollo capsule in a suborbital flight. Two more flights followed in quick succession. Then there was a hiatus of more than a year before the 22 January 1968 launch of a *Saturn IB* with both an Apollo capsule and a lunar landing module aboard for orbital testing. The only astronaut-occupied flight of the *Saturn IB* took place between 11 and 22 October 1968 when Walter Schirra, Donn F. Eisele, and R. Walter Cunningham, made 163 orbits testing Apollo equipment.[70]

The largest launch vehicle of this family, the *Saturn V*, represented the culmination of those earlier booster development and test programs. Standing 363 feet tall, with three stages, this was the vehicle that could take astronauts to the Moon and return them safely to Earth. The first stage generated 7.5 million pounds of thrust from five massive engines developed for the system. These engines, known as the F-1, were some of the most significant engineering accomplishments of the program, requiring the development of new alloys and different construction techniques to withstand the extreme heat and shock of firing. The thunderous sound of the first static test of this stage, taking place at Huntsville, Alabama, on 16 April 1965, brought home to many that the Kennedy goal was within technological grasp. For others, it signaled the magic of technological effort; one engineer even characterized rocket engine technology as a "black art" without rational principles. The second stage presented enormous challenges to NASA engineers and very nearly caused the lunar landing goal to be missed. Consisting of five engines burning LOX and liquid hydrogen, this stage could deliver 1 million pounds of

Apollo 11 third stage (S-1VB) is being raised for mating to the second stage. NASA Photo #69-H-321.

thrust. It was always behind schedule, and required constant attention and additional funding to ensure completion by the deadline for a lunar landing. Both the first and third stages of this Saturn vehicle development program moved forward relatively smoothly. (The third stage was an enlarged and improved version of the IB, and had few developmental complications.)[71]

Despite all of this, the biggest problem with *Saturn V* lay not with the hardware, but with the clash of philosophies toward development and test. The von Braun "Rocket Team" had made important technological contributions and enjoyed popular acclaim as a result of conservative engineering practices that took minutely incremental approaches toward test and verification. They tested each component of each system individually and then assembled them for a long series of ground tests. Then they would launch each stage individually before assembling the whole system for a long series of flight tests. While this practice ensured thoroughness, it was both costly and time-consuming, and NASA had neither commodity to expend. George E. Mueller, the head of NASA's Office of Manned Space Flight, dis-

agreed with this approach. Drawing on his experience with the Air Force and aerospace industry, and shadowed by the twin bugaboos of schedule and cost, Mueller advocated what he called the "all-up" concept in which the entire Apollo-Saturn system was tested together in flight without the laborious preliminaries.[72]

A calculated gamble, the first *Saturn V* test launch took place on 9 November 1967 with the entire Apollo-Saturn combination. A second test followed on 4 April 1968, and even though it was only partially successful because the second stage shut off prematurely and the third stage—needed to start the Apollo payload into lunar trajectory—failed, Mueller declared that the test program had been completed and that the next launch would have astronauts aboard. The gamble paid off. In 17 test and 15 piloted launches, the Saturn booster family scored a 100 percent launch reliability rate.[73]

THE APOLLO SPACECRAFT

Almost with the announcement of the lunar landing commitment in 1961 NASA technicians began a crash program to develop a reasonable configuration for the trip to lunar orbit and back. What they came up with was a three-person command module capable of sustaining human life for two weeks or more in either Earth orbit or in a lunar trajectory; a service module holding oxygen, fuel, maneuvering rockets, fuel cells, and other expendable and life support equipment that could be jettisoned upon reentry to Earth; a retrorocket package attached to the service module for slowing to prepare for reentry; and finally a launch escape system that was discarded upon achieving orbit. The tear-drop shaped command module had two hatches, one on the side for entry and exit of the crew at the beginning and end of the flight and one in the nose with a docking collar for use in moving to and from the lunar landing vehicle.[74]

Work on the Apollo spacecraft stretched from 28 November 1961, when the prime contract for its development was let to North American Aviation, to 22 October 1968 when the last test flight took place. In between there were various efforts to design, build, and test the spacecraft both on the ground and in suborbital and orbital flights. For instance, on 13 May 1964 NASA tested a boilerplate model of the Apollo capsule atop a stubby *Little Joe II* military booster, and another Apollo capsule actually achieved orbit on 18 September 1964 when it was launched atop a *Saturn I*. By the end of 1966 NASA leaders declared the Apollo command module ready for human occupancy. The final flight checkout of the spacecraft prior to the lunar flight took place on 11–22 October 1968 with three astronauts.[75]

As these development activities were taking place, tragedy struck the Apollo program. On 27 January 1967, Apollo-Saturn (AS) 204, scheduled to be the first spaceflight with astronauts aboard the capsule, was on the launch pad at Kennedy Space Center, Florida, moving through simulation tests. The three astronauts to fly on this mission—"Gus" Grissom, Edward White, and Roger B. Chaffee—were aboard running through a mock launch sequence. At 6:31 p.m., after several hours of work, a fire broke out in the spacecraft and the pure oxygen atmosphere intended for the flight helped it burn with intensity. In a flash, flames engulfed the capsule and the astronauts died of asphyxiation. It took the ground crew five minutes to open the hatch. When they did so they found three bodies. Although three other astronauts had been killed before this time—all in plane crashes—these were the first deaths directly attributable to the U.S. space program.[76]

Shock gripped NASA and the nation during the days that followed. James Webb, NASA Administrator, told the media at the time, "We've always known that something like this was going to happen sooner or later . . . who would have thought that the first tragedy would be on the ground?"[77] As the nation mourned, Webb went to President Lyndon Johnson and asked that NASA be allowed to handle the accident investigation and direct the recovery from the accident. He promised to be truthful in assessing blame and pledged to assign it to himself and NASA management as appropriate. The day after the fire NASA appointed an eight member investigation board, chaired by longtime NASA official and director of the Langley Research Center, Floyd L. Thompson. It set out to discover the details of the tragedy: what happened, why it happened, could it happen again, what was at fault, and how could NASA recover? The members of the board learned that the fire had been caused by a short circuit in the electrical system that ignited combustible materials in the spacecraft fed by the oxygen atmosphere. They also found that it could have been prevented and called for several modifications to the spacecraft, including a move to a less oxygen-rich environment. Changes to the capsule followed quickly, and within a little more than a year it was ready for flight.[78]

Webb reported these findings to various Congressional committees and took a personal grilling at every meeting. His answers were sometimes evasive and always defensive. The *New York Times,* which was usually critical of Webb, had a field day with this situation and said that NASA stood for "Never a Straight

The Apollo 11 spacecraft and booster at Launch Complex 39A in preparation for the first lunar mission in July 1969. NASA Photo #69-H-1051.

Answer." While the ordeal was personally taxing, whether by happenstance or design Webb deflected much of the backlash over the fire from both NASA as an agency and from the Johnson administration. While he was personally tarred with the disaster, the space agency's image and popular support was largely undamaged. Webb himself never recovered from the stigma of the fire, and when he left NASA in October 1968, even as Apollo was nearing a successful completion, few mourned his departure.[79]

The AS 204 fire also troubled Webb ideologically during the months that followed. He had been a high priest of technocracy ever since coming to NASA in 1961, arguing for the authority of experts, well-organized and led, and with sufficient resources to resolve the "many great economic, social, and political problems" that pressed the nation. He wrote in his book, *Space Age Management,* as late as 1969 that "Our Society has reached a point where its progress and even its survival increasingly depend upon our ability to organize the complex and to do the unusual."[80] He believed he had achieved that model organization for complex accomplishments at NASA. Yet that model structure of exemplary management had failed to anticipate and resolve the shortcomings in the Apollo capsule design and had not taken what seemed in retrospect to be normal precautions to ensure the safety of the crew. The system had broken down. As a result Webb became less trustful of other officials at NASA and gathered more and more decisionmaking authority to himself. This wore on him during the rest of his time as NASA Administrator, and in reality the failure of the technological model for solving problems was an important forecaster of a trend that would be increasingly present in American culture thereafter as technology was blamed for a good many of society's ills. That problem would be particularly present as NASA tried to win political approval of later NASA projects.[81]

THE LUNAR MODULE

If the Saturn launch vehicle and the Apollo spacecraft were difficult technological challenges, the third part of the hardware for the Moon landing, the Lunar

Module (LM), represented the most serious problem. Begun a year later than it should have been, the LM was consistently behind schedule and over budget. Much of the problem turned on the demands of devising two separate spacecraft components—one for descent to the Moon and one for ascent back to the command module—that only maneuvered outside an atmosphere. Both engines had to work perfectly or the very real possibility existed that the astronauts would not return home. Guidance, maneuverability, and spacecraft control also caused no end of headaches. The landing structure likewise presented problems; it had to be light and sturdy and shock resistent. An ungainly vehicle emerged which two astronauts could fly while standing. In November 1962 Grumman Aerospace Corp. signed a contract with NASA to produce the LM, and work on it began in earnest. With difficulty the LM was orbited on a *Saturn V* test launch in January 1968 and judged ready for operation.[82]

TRIPS TO THE MOON

After a piloted orbital mission to test the Apollo equipment on October 1968, on 21 December 1968 *Apollo 8* took off atop a *Saturn V* booster from the

Mission control at the Manned Spacecraft Center at Houston, Texas, during Project Apollo. NASA Photo #S-69-39593.

Kennedy Space Center with three astronauts aboard—Frank Borman, James A. Lovell, Jr., and William A. Anders—for a historic mission to orbit the Moon.[83] At first it was planned as a mission to test Apollo hardware in the relatively safe confines of low Earth orbit, but senior engineer George M. Low of the Manned Spacecraft Center at Houston, Texas, and Samuel C. Phillips, Apollo Program Manager at NASA headquarters, pressed for approval to make it a circumlunar flight. The advantages of this could be important, both in technical and scientific knowledge gained as well as in a public demonstration of what the U.S. could achieve.[84] So far Apollo had been all promise; now the delivery was about to begin. In the summer of 1968 Low broached the idea to Phillips, who then carried it to the administrator, and in November the agency reconfigured the mission for a lunar trip. After *Apollo 8* made one and a half Earth orbits its third stage began a burn to put the spacecraft on a lunar trajectory. As it traveled outward the crew focused a portable television camera on Earth and for the first time humanity saw its home from afar, a tiny, lovely, and fragile "blue marble" hanging in the blackness of space. When it arrived at the Moon on Christmas Eve this image of Earth was even more strongly reinforced when the crew sent images of the planet back while reading the first part of the Bible—"And God created the heavens and the Earth, and the Earth was without form and void"—before sending Christmas greetings to humanity. The next day they fired the boosters for a return flight and "spashed down" in the Pacific Ocean on 27 December. It was an enormously significant accomplishment coming at a time when American society was in crisis over Vietnam, race relations, urban problems, and a host of other difficulties. And if only for a few moments the nation united as one to focus on this epochal event. Two more Apollo missions occurred before the climax of the program, but they did little more than confirm that the time had come for a lunar landing.[85]

Then came the big event. *Apollo 11* lifted off on 16 July 1969, and after confirming that the hardware was working well began the three day trip to the Moon. At 4:18 p.m. EST on 20 July 1969 the LM—with astronauts Neil A. Armstrong and Edwin E. Aldrin—landed on the lunar surface while Michael Collins orbited overhead in the Apollo command module. After checkout, Armstrong set foot on the surface, telling millions who saw and heard him on Earth that it was "one small step for man—one giant leap for mankind." (Neil Armstrong later added "a" when referring to "one small step for *a* man" to clarify the

first sentence delivered from the Moon's surface.) Aldrin soon followed him out, and the two plodded around the landing site in the 1/6 lunar gravity, planted an American flag but omitted claiming the land for the U.S. as had been routinely done during European exploration of the Americas, collected soil and rock samples, and set up scientific experiments. The next day they launched back to the Apollo capsule orbiting overhead and began the return trip to Earth, splashing down in the Pacific on 24 July.[86]

The footprint on the Moon, July 1969. NASA Photo #69-H-1259.

These flights rekindled the excitement felt in the early 1960s with John Glenn and the Mercury astronauts. *Apollo 11*, in particular, met with an ecstatic reaction around the globe, as everyone shared in the success of the mission. Ticker tape parades, speaking engagements, public relations events, and a world tour by the astronauts served to create good will both in the U.S. and abroad.

Five more landing missions followed at approximately six month intervals through December 1972, each of them increasing the time spent on the Moon. Three of the latter Apollo missions used a lunar rover vehicle to travel in the vicinity of the landing site, but none of them equaled the excitement of *Apollo 11*. The scientific experiments placed on the Moon and the lunar soil samples returned through Project Apollo have provided grist for scientists' investigations of the Solar System ever since. The scientific return was significant, but the Apollo program did not answer conclusively the age-old questions of lunar origins and evolution.[87]

In spite of the success of the other missions, only *Apollo 13*, launched on 11 April 1970, came close to matching earlier popular interest. But that was only because, 56 hours into the flight, an oxygen tank in the

Apollo service module ruptured and damaged several of the power, electrical, and life support systems. People throughout the world watched and waited and hoped as NASA personnel on the ground and the crew, well in their way to the Moon and with no way of returning until they went around it, worked together to find a way safely home. While NASA engineers quickly determined that air, water, and electricity did not exist in the Apollo capsule sufficient to sustain the three astronauts until they could return to Earth, they found that the LM—a self-contained spacecraft unaffected by the accident—could be used as a "lifeboat" to provide austere life support for the return trip. It was a close-run thing, but the crew returned safely on 17 April 1970. The near disaster served several important purposes for the civil space program—especially prompting reconsideration of the propriety of the whole effort while also solidifying in the popular mind NASA's technological genius.[88]

A Meaning for Apollo

Project Apollo in general, and the flight of *Apollo 11* in particular, should be viewed as a watershed in the nation's history. It was an endeavor that demonstrated both the technological and economic virtuosity of the United States and established technologically preeminence over rival nations—the primary goal of the program when first envisioned by the Kennedy administration in 1961. It had been an enormous undertaking, costing $25.4 billion (about $95 billion in 1990 dollars), with only the building of the Panama Canal rivaling the Apollo program's size as the largest non-military technological endeavor ever undertaken by the United States and only the Manhattan Project to build the atomic bomb in World War II being comparable in a wartime setting.

There are several important legacies (or conclusions) about Project Apollo that need to be remembered. First, and probably most important, the Apollo program was successful in accomplishing the political goals for which it had been created. Kennedy had been dealing with a Cold War crisis in 1961 brought on by several separate factors—the Soviet orbiting of Yuri Gagarin and the disastrous Bay of Pigs invasion only two of them—that Apollo was designed to combat. At the time of the *Apollo 11* landing Mission Control in Houston flashed the words of President Kennedy announcing the Apollo commitment on its big screen.

A ticker-tape parade for the Apollo 11 astronauts in New York City. NASA Photo #69-H-1420.

Those phrases were followed with these: "TASK ACCOMPLISHED, July 1969." No greater understatement could probably have been made. Any assessment of Apollo that does not recognize the accomplishment of landing an American on the Moon and safely returning before the end of the 1960s is incomplete and innaccurate, for that was the primary goal of the undertaking.[89]

Second, Project Apollo was a triumph of management in meeting enormously difficult systems engineering, technological, and organizational integration requirements. James E. Webb, the NASA Administrator at the height of the program between 1961 and 1968, always contended that Apollo was much more a management exercise than anything else, and that the technological challenge, while sophisticated and impressive, was largely within grasp at the time of the 1961 decision.[90] More difficult was ensuring that those technological skills were properly managed and used.

Webb's contention was confirmed in spades by the success of Apollo. NASA leaders had to acquire and organize unprecedented resources to accomplish the task at hand. From both a political and technological perspective, management was critical. For seven years after Kennedy's Apollo decision, through October 1968, James Webb maneuvered for NASA in Washington to obtain sufficient resources to meet Apollo requirements. More to the point, NASA personnel employed the "program management" concept that centralized authority and emphasized systems engineering. The systems management of the program was critical to Apollo's success.[91] Understanding the management of complex structures for the successful completion of a multifarious task was a critical outgrowth of the Apollo effort.

Third, Project Apollo forced the people of the world to view the planet Earth in a new way. *Apollo 8* was critical to this fundamental change, as it treated the world to the first pictures of the Earth from afar. Writer Archibald MacLeish summed up the feelings of many people when he wrote at the time of Apollo, that "To see the Earth as it truly is, small and blue and beautiful in that eternal silence where it floats, is to see ourselves as riders on the Earth together, brothers on that bright loveliness in the eternal cold—brothers who know now that they are truly brothers."[92] The modern environmental movement was galvanized in part by this new perception of the planet and the need to protect it and the life that it supports.[93]

Finally, the Apollo program, while an enormous achievement, left a divided legacy for NASA and the

During a later Apollo flight, astronauts employed the Lunar Rover. This photograph is from the Apollo 15 mission of July–August 1971. NASA Photo #71-H-1286.

aerospace community. The perceived "golden age" of Apollo created for the agency an expectation that the direction of any major space goal from the president would always bring NASA a broad consensus of support and provide it with the resources and license to dispense them as it saw fit. Something most NASA officials did not understand at the time of the Moon landing in 1969, however, was that Apollo had not been conducted under normal political circumstances and that the exceptional circumstances surrounding Apollo would not be repeated.[94]

The Apollo decision was, therefore, an anomaly in the national decision-making process. The dilemma of the "golden age" of Apollo has been difficult to overcome, but moving beyond the Apollo program to embrace future opportunities has been an important goal of the agency's leadership in the recent past. Exploration of the Solar System and the universe remains as enticing a goal and as important an objective for humanity as it ever has been. Project Apollo was an important early step in that ongoing process of exploration.

NOTES

[1] Michael R. Beschloss, *The Crisis Years: Kennedy and Khrushchev, 1960-1963* (New York: Harper, 1991), p. 28; U.S. Senate, *Joint Appearances of Senator John F. Kennedy and Vice President Richard M. Nixon* (Washington, DC: U.S. Government Printing Office, 1961); U.S. Senate, *The Speeches of Senator John F. Kennedy: Presidential Campaign of 1960* (Washington, DC: U.S. Government Printing Office, 1961).

[2] See John M. Logsdon, "An Apollo Perspective," *Astronautics & Aeronautics,* December 1979, pp. 112-17.

[3] Jerome B. Wiesner, "Report to the President-elect of the Ad Hoc Committee on Space," 12 January 1961, p. 16, Presidential Papers, John F. Kennedy Presidential Library, Boston, MA.

[4] On this see Loyd S. Swenson, Jr., James M. Grimwood, and Charles C. Alexander, *This New Ocean: A History of Project Mercury* (Washington, DC: NASA SP-4201, 1966), 129-32.

[5] Wiesner, "Report to the President-elect," 12 January 1961, p. 16.

[6] "Inaugural Address, January 20, 1961," in *Public Papers of the Presidents of the United States: John F. Kennedy, 1961* (Washington, DC: Government Printing Office, 1962), pp. 1-3.

[7] "Annual Message to the Congress on the State of the Union, January 30, 1961," in ibid., pp. 19-28, quote from p. 26.

[8] Arnold W. Frutkin oral history, April 4, 1974, by Eugene M. Emme and Alex Roland, pp. 28-29, and Arnold W. Frutkin oral history, July 30, 1970, by John M. Logsdon, pp. 17-18, both in NASA Historical Reference Collection, NASA Headquarters, Washington, DC. See also Arnold W. Frutkin, *International Cooperation in Space* (Englewood Cliffs, NJ: Prentice-Hall, 1965).

[9] Quoted in John M. Logsdon, *The Decision to Go to the Moon: Project Apollo and the National Interest* (Cambridge, MA: MIT Press, 1970), p. 111.

[10] David Bell, Memorandum for the President, "National Aeronautics and Space Administration Budget Problem," 22 March 1961, NASA Historical Reference Collection; U.S. Congress, House, Committee of Science and Astronautics, *NASA Fiscal 1962 Authorization, Hearings,* 87th Cong., 1st. sess., 1962, pp. 203, 620; Logsdon, *Decision to Go to the Moon,* pp. 94-100.

[11] Leonid Vladimirov, *The Russian Space Bluff: The Inside Story of the Soviet Drive to the Moon* (New York: Dial Press, 1973), trans. David Floyd, pp. 86-97; *Pravda,* 17 April 1961, 12 May 1961; Walter A. McDougall, . . . *The Heavens and The Earth: A Political History of the Space Age* (New York: Basic Books, 1985), pp. 243-49; Brian Harvey, *Race into Space: The Soviet Space Programme* (London: Ellis Horwood, 1988), pp. 38-59; Swenson, Grimwood, and Alexander, *This New Ocean,* pp. 341-81.

[12] *New York Times,* 17 April 1961, p. 5.

[13] On this invasion see, Peter Wyden, *Bay of Pigs: The Untold Story* (New York: Simon and Schuster, 1979); Haynes Bonner Johnson, *The Bay of Pigs: The Leaders' Story of Brigade 2506* (New York: W.W. Norton and Co., 1964); Albert C. Persons, *Bay of Pigs: A Firsthand Account of the Mission by a U.S. Pilot in Support of the Cuban Invasion Force in 1961* (Jefferson, NC: McFarland, 1990).

[14] Quoted in Logsdon, *Decision to Go to the Moon,* pp. 111-12.

[15] T. Keith Glennan, *The Birth of NASA: The Diary of T. Keith Glennan,* edited by J.D. Hunley (Washington, DC: NASA SP-4105, 1993), pp. 314-15. This is essentially the same position as set forth in Logsdon, *Decision to Go to the Moon,* pp. 111-12, although McDougall, . . . *Heavens and the Earth,* p. 8, also includes a "growing technocratic mentality" as a reason for the decision.

[16] John F. Kennedy, Memorandum for Vice President, 20 April 1961, Presidential Files, John F. Kennedy Presidential Library, Boston, MA.

[17] *New York Times,* 22 April 1961.

[18] Logsdon, "An Apollo Perspective," p. 114.

[19] Hugh L. Dryden to Lyndon B. Johnson, 22 April 1961, Vice Presidential Security File, box 17, John F. Kennedy Library; Logsdon, *Decision to Go to the Moon,* pp. 59-61, 112-14.

[20] Wernher von Braun to Lyndon B. Johnson, 29 April 1961, NASA Historical Reference Collection.

[21] Robert A. Divine, "Lyndon B. Johnson and the Politics of Space," in Robert A. Divine, ed., *The Johnson Years: Vietnam, the Environment, and Science* (Lawrence: University Press of Kansas, 1987), pp. 231-33.

[22] Quoted in Logsdon, *Decision to Go to the Moon,* p. 115.

[23] This letter is printed in U.S. Congress, Senate, Committee on Aeronautical and Space Sciences, *NASA Authorization for Fiscal Year 1962,* 87th Cong., 1st sess. (Washington, DC: Government Printing Office, 1961), p. 257.

[24] Edward C. Welsh Oral History, pp. 11-12, Lyndon B. Johnson Presidential Library, Austin, TX.

[25] Lyndon B. Johnson, Vice President, Memorandum for the President, "Evaluation of Space Program," April 28, 1961, Presidential Papers, Kennedy Presidential Library.

[26] James E. Webb to Jerome B. Wiesner, 2 May 1961, NASA Historical Reference Collection.

[27] James E. Webb and Robert S. McNamara to John F. Kennedy, May 8, 1961, John F. Kennedy Library.

[28] There is evidence to suggest that the 1967 date was hit upon because it was the fiftieth anniversary of the communist revolution in the Soviet Union and that U.S. leaders believed the Soviets were planning something spectacular in space in commemoration of the date. Interview with Robert C. Seamans, Jr., 23 February 1994, Washington, DC.

[29] See original excerpts from "Urgent National Needs," Speech to a Joint Session of Congress, 25 May 1961, Presidential Files, Kennedy Presidential Library.

[30] John F. Kennedy, "Urgent National Needs," *Congressional Record—House* (25 May 1961), p. 8276; text of speech, speech files, NASA Historical Reference Collection, NASA History Office, Washington, DC.

[31] Logsdon, "An Apollo Perspective," p. 115.

[32] John Law, "Technology and Heterogeneous Engineering: The Case of Portuguese Expansion," pp. 111-34; and Donald MacKenzie, "Missile Accuracy: A Case Study in the Social Processes of Technological Change," pp. 195-222, both in Wiebe E. Bijker, Thomas P. Hughes, and Trevor J. Pinch, eds., *The Social Construction of Technological Systems: New Directions in the Sociology and History of Technology* (Cambridge, MA: The MIT Press, 1987).

[33] As an example see the 1963 defense of Apollo by the vice president. Vice President Lyndon B. Johnson to the President, 13 May 1963, with attached report, John F. Kennedy Presidential Files, NASA Historical Reference Collection.

[34] Linda Neuman Ezell, *NASA Historical Data Book, Vol II: Programs and Projects, 1958-1968* (Washington, DC: NASA SP-4012, 1988), pp. 122-23.

[35] *Aeronautics and Space Report of the President, 1988 Activities* (Washington, DC: NASA Annual Report, 1990), p. 185.

[36] Ezell, *NASA Historical Data Book, Vol II,* 2:122-32.

[37] On Webb see, W. Henry Lambright, *Powering Apollo: James E. Webb of NASA* (Baltimore, MD: Johns Hopkins University Press, 1995).

[38] On this subject see Arnold S. Levine, *Managing NASA in the Apollo Era* (Washington, DC: NASA SP-4102, 1982), Chapter 4.

[39] See Sylvia K. Kraemer, "Organizing for Exploration," in John M. Logsdon, editor. *Exploring the Unknown: Selected Documents in the History of the U.S. Civil Space Program, Volume I, Organizing for Exploration* (Washington, DC: NASA SP-4407, 1995), chapter 4.

[40] On these see, Virginia P. Dawson, *Engines and Innovation: Lewis Laboratory and American Propulsion Technology* (Washington, DC: NASA SP-4306, 1991); James R. Hansen, *Engineer in Charge: A History of the Langley Aeronautical Laboratory, 1917-1958* (Washington, DC: NASA SP-4305, 1987); Elizabeth A. Muenger, *Searching the Horizon: A History of Ames Research Center, 1940-1976* (Washington, DC: NASA SP-4304, 1985); Richard P. Hallion, *On the Frontier: Flight Research at Dryden, 1946-1981* (Washington, DC: NASA SP-4303, 1984); Alfred Rosenthal, *Venture into Space: Early Years of Goddard Space Flight Center* (Washington, DC: NASA SP-4301, 1968); Clayton R. Koppes, *JPL and the American Space Program: A History of the Jet Propulsion Laboratory* (New Haven, CT: Yale University Press, 1982); Henry C. Dethloff, *"Suddenly Tomorrow Came . . .": A History of the Johnson Space Center* (Washington, DC: NASA SP-4307; and Charles D. Benson and William Barnaby Faherty, *Moonport: A History of Apollo Launch Facilities and Operations* (Washington, DC: NASA SP-4204, 1978).

[41] On the NASA organizational culture see, Howard E. McCurdy, *Inside NASA: High Technology and Organizational Change in the U.S. Space Program* (Baltimore, MD: Johns Hopkins University Press, 1993).

[42] Albert F. Siepert, memorandum to James E. Webb, 8 February 1963, NASA Historical Reference Collection; Sarah M. Turner, "Sam Phillips: One Who Led Us to the Moon," *NASA Activities,* 21 (May/June 1990): 18-19.

[43] Aaron Cohen, "Project Management: JSC's Heritage and Challenge," *Issues in NASA Program and Project Management* (Washington, DC: NASA SP-6101, 1989), pp. 7-16; C. Thomas Newman, "Controlling Resources in the Apollo Program," *Issues in NASA Program and Project Management* (Washington, DC: NASA SP-6101, 1989), pp. 23-26; Eberhard Rees, "Project and Systems Management in the Apollo Program," *Issues in NASA Program and Project Management* (Washington, DC: NASA SP-6101 (02), 1989), pp. 24-34.

[44] Dael Wolfe, Executive Officer, American Association for the Advancement of Science, editorial for *Science*, 15 November 1968.

[45] Roger E. Bilstein, *Stages to Saturn: A Technological History of the Apollo/Saturn Launch Vehicles* (Washington, DC: NASA SP-4206, 1980), *passim*, and Appendix E.

[46] McCurdy, *Inside NASA*, pp. 11-98.

[47] See the discussion of this issue in Sylvia Doughty Fries, "Apollo: A Pioneering Generation," International Astronautical Federation, 37th Congress, 9 October 1986, Ref. No. IAA-86-495; Sylvia Doughty Fries, *NASA Engineers and the Age of Apollo* (Washington, DC: NASA SP-4104, 1992), passim.

[48] Eberhard Rees, memorandum, 9 December 1965, quoted in Bilstein, *Stages to Saturn,* p. 227; interview with John D. Young by Howard E. McCurdy, 19 August 1987, NASA Historical Reference Collection.

[49] This story has been told in John M. Logsdon, "Selecting the Way to the Moon: The Choice of the Lunar Orbital Rendezvous Mode," *Aerospace Historian,* 18 (Summer 1971): 63-70; Courtney G. Brooks, James M. Grimwood, and Loyd S. Swenson, Jr., *Chariots for Apollo: A History of Manned Lunar Spacecraft* (Washington: NASA SP-4205, 1979), pp. 61-86; Bilstein, *Stages to Saturn,* pp. 57-68; and James R. Hansen, "Enchanted Rendezvous: The Genesis of the Lunar-Orbit Rendezvous Concept," 1993, unpublished historical manuscript, NASA Historical Reference Collection.

[50] John C. Houbolt, "Lunar Rendezvous," *International Science and Technology,* 14 (February 1963): 62-65.

[51] "Concluding Remarks by Dr. Wernher von Braun about Mode Selection given to Dr. Joseph F. Shea, Deputy Director (Systems), Office of Manned Space Flight," 7 June 1962, NASA Historical Reference Collection.

[52] Quoted in Charles A. Murray and Catherine Bly Cox, *Apollo, the Race to the Moon* (New York: Simon and Schuster, 1989), pp. 142-43.

[53] Brooks, Grimwood, and Swenson, *Chariots for Apollo,* pp. 106-107.

[54] Swenson, Grimwood, and Alexander, *This New Ocean,* pp. 341-79.

[55] Wernher von Braun, "The Redstone, Jupiter, and Juno," in Eugene M. Emme, ed., *The History of Rocket Technology: Essays on Research, Development, and Utility* (Detroit: Wayne State University Press, 1964), pp. 107-22.

[56] See Richard E. Martin, *The Atlas and Centaur "Steel Balloon" Tanks: A Legacy of Karel Bossart* (San Diego, CA: General Dynamics Space Systems Division, 1989).

[57] Interview with Karrel J. Bossart by John L. Sloop, 27 April 1974, quoted in John L. Sloop, *Liquid Hydrogen as a Propulsion Fuel, 1945-1959* (Washington, DC: NASA SP-4404, 1978), pp. 176-77.

[58] Martin, *Atlas and Centaur "Steel Balloon" Tanks,* p. 5.

[59] Swenson, Grimwood, and Alexander, *This New Ocean,* pp. 422-36.

[60] *Ibid.,* pp. 446-503.

[61] Barton C. Hacker, "The Idea of Rendezvous: From Space Station to Orbital Operations, in Space-Travel Thought, 1895-1951," *Technology and Culture,* 15 (July 1974): 373-88; Barton C. Hacker, "The Genesis of Project Apollo: The Idea of Rendezvous, 1929-1961," *Actes 10: Historic des techniques* (Paris: Congress of the History of Science, 1971), pp. 41-46; Barton C. Hacker and James M. Grimwood, *On Shoulders of Titans: A History of Project Gemini* (Washington, DC: NASA SP-4203, 1977), pp. 1-26.

[62] James M. Grimwood and Ivan D. Ertal, "Project Gemini," *Southwestern Historical Quarterly,* 81 (January 1968): 393-418; James M. Grimwood, Barton C. Hacker, and Peter J. Vorzimmer, *Project Gemini Technology and Operations* (Washington, DC: NASA SP-4002, 1969); Robert N. Lindley, "Discussing Gemini: A 'Flight' Interview with Robert Lindley of McDonnell," *Flight International,* 24 March 1966, pp. 488-89.

[63] Reginald M. Machell, ed., *Summary of Gemini Extravehicular Activity* (Washington, DC: NASA SP-149, 1968).

[64] *Gemini Summary Conference* (Washington, DC: NASA SP-138, 1967); Ezell, *NASA Historical Data Book, Vol. II,* pp. 149-70.

[65] On this project see, R. Cargill Hall, *Lunar Impact: A History of Project Ranger* (Washington, DC: NASA SP-4210, 1977).

[66] On this project see, Bruce K. Byers, *Destination Moon: A History of the Lunar Orbiter Program* (Washington, DC: NASA TM X-3487, 1977).

[67] Surveyor's history has yet to be written, but a start is contained in Ezell, *NASA Historical Data Book, Vol. II,* pp. 325-31.

[68] U.S. Senate Committee on Aeronautical and Space Sciences, NASA Authorization Subcommittee, *Transfer of Von Braun Team to NASA, 86th Cong., 2d*

Sess. (Washington, DC: Government Printing Office, 1960); Robert M. Rosholt, *An Administrative History of NASA, 1958-1963* (Washington, DC: NASA SP-4101, 1966), pp. 46-47, 117-20.

[69] Bilstein, *Stages to Saturn*, pp. 155-258; Ezell, *NASA Historical Data Book, Vol. II*, pp. 54-61.

[70] Ezell, *NASA Historical Data Book, Vol. II*, pp. 58-59.

[71] Roger E. Bilstein, "From the S-IV to the S-IVB: The Evolution of a Rocket Stage for Space Exploration," *Journal of the British Interplanetary Society,* 32 (December 1979): 452-58; Richard P. Hallion, "The Development of American Launch Vehicles since 1945," in Paul A. Hanle ad Vol Del Chamberlain," eds., *Space Science Comes of Age: Perspectives in the History of the Space Sciences* (Washington, DC: Smithsonian Institution Press, 1981), pp. 126-32.

[72] George E. Mueller, NASA, to Manned Spacecraft Center Director, *et al.*, 31 October 1963; Eberhard Rees, Marshall Space Flight Center Director, to Robert Sherrod, 4 March 1970, both in "Saturn 'All-Up' Testing Concept" File, Launch Vehicles, NASA Historical Reference Collection; Bilstein, *Stages to Saturn*, pp. 348-51; McCurdy, *Inside NASA*, pp. 94-96, Murray and Cox, *Apollo*, pp. 160-62.

[73] Ezell, *NASA Historical Data Book, Vol. II*, p. 61; *Space Flight: The First Thirty Years* (Washington, DC: NASA NP-150, 1991), pp. 12-17.

[74] A lengthy discussion of the development of the Apollo spacecraft can be found in Ivan D. Ertal and Mary Louise Morse, *The Apollo Spacecraft: A Chronology, Volume I, Through November 7, 1962* (Washington, DC: NASA SP-4009, 1969); Mary Louise Morse and Jean Kernahan Bays, *The Apollo Spacecraft: A Chronology, Volume II, November 8, 1962-September 30, 1964* (Washington, DC: NASA SP-4009, 1973); Courtney G. Brooks and Ivan D. Ertal, *The Apollo Spacecraft: A Chronology, Volume III, October 1, 1964-January 20, 1966* (Washington, DC: NASA SP-4009, 1973); and Ivan D. Ertal and Roland W. Newkirk, with Courtney G. Brooks, *The Apollo Spacecraft: A Chronology, Volume IV, January 21, 1966-July 13, 1974* (Washington, DC: NASA SP-4009, 1978). A short developmental history is in Ezell, *NASA Historical Data Book, Vol. II*, pp. 171-85.

[75] Ezell, *NASA Historical Data Book, Vol. II*, pp. 182-85.

[76] On this subject see, "The Ten Desperate Minutes," *Life,* 21 April 1967, pp. 113-114; Erik Bergaust, *Murder on Pad 34* (New York: G.P. Putnam's Sons, 1968); Mike Gray, *Angle of Attack: Harrison Storms and the Race to the Moon* (New York: W.W. Norton and Co., 1992);

Erlend A. Kennan and Edmund H. Harvey, Jr., *Mission to the Moon: A Critical Examination of NASA and the Space Program* (New York: William Morrow and Co., 1969); Hugo Young, Bryan Silcock, and Peter Dunn, *Journey to Tranquillity: The History of Man's Assault on the Moon* (Garden City, NY: Doubleday, 1970); Brooks, Grimwood, and Swenson, *Chariots for Apollo,* pp. 213-36.

[77] Quoted in Bergaust, *Murder on Pad 34,* p. 23.

[78] United States House, Committee on Science and Astronautics, Subcommittee on NASA Oversight, *Investigation into Apollo 204 accident, Hearings, Ninetieth Congress, first session* (Washington, DC: Government Printing Office, 1967); United States House, Committee on Science and Astronautics, *Apollo Program Pace and Progress; Staff Study for the Subcommittee on NASA Oversight, Ninetieth Congress, first session* (Washington, DC: Government Printing Office, 1967); United States House, Committee on Science and Aeronautics, *Apollo and Apollo Applications: Staff Study for the Subcommittee on NASA Oversight of the Committee on Science and Astronautics, U.S. House of Representatives, Ninetieth Congress, Second Session* (Washington, DC: Government Printing Office, 1968); Robert C. Seamans, Jr., and Frederick I. Ordway III, "Lessons of Apollo for Large-Scale Technology," in Frederick C. Durant III, ed., *Between Sputnik and the Shuttle: New Perspectives on American Astronautics* (San Diego: Univelt, 1981), pp. 241-87.

[79] Administrative History of NASA, chap. II, pp. 47-52, Administrative Files, Lyndon B. Johnson Presidential Library, Austin, TX; Lyndon B. Johnson interview by Walter Cronkite 5 July 1969, LBJ Files, Johnson Presidential Library; Senator Clinton P. Anderson by Robert Sherrod, 25 July 1968; Sherrod to John B. Oakes, May 24, 1972, RSAC; Edward C. Welsh interview by Eugene M. Emme, 20 February 1969, all in NASA Historical Reference Collection; Lambright, *Powering Apollo,* chapter 9.

[80] James E. Webb, *Space Age Management: The Large Scale Approach* (New York: McGraw-Hill Book Co., 1969), p. 15.

[81] Interview with Robert C. Seamans, Jr., 23 February 1994, Washington, DC.

[82] Ezell, *NASA Historical Data Book, Vol. II*, pp. 173-76, 187-94.

[83] *Space Flight: The First 30 Years,* p. 14.

[84] NASA, Apollo Program Director, to NASA, Associate Administrator for Manned Space Flight, "Apollo 8 Mission Selection," 11 November 1968, Apollo 8 Files, NASA Historical Reference Collection.

[85] Rene Jules Dubos, *A Theology of the Earth* (Washington, DC: Smithsonian Institution, 1969), pp. 1-3; Oran W. Nicks, ed., *This Island Earth* (Washington, DC: NASA SP-250, 1970), pp. 3-4; R. Cargill Hall, "Project Apollo in Retrospect," 20 June 1990, pp. 25-26, R. Cargill Hall Biographical File, NASA Historical Reference Collection.

[86] Neil A. Armstrong, *et al., First on the Moon: A Voyage with Neil Armstrong, Michael Collins and Edwin E. Aldrin, Jr.,* Written with Gene Farmer and Dora Jane Hamblin (Boston: Little, Brown, 1970); Neil A. Armstrong, *et al., The First Lunar Landing: 20th Anniversary/as Told by the Astronauts, Neil Armstrong, Edwin Aldrin, Michael Collins* (Washington, DC: NASA EP-73, 1989); John Barbour, *Footprints on the Moon* (Washington, DC: The Associated Press, 1969); CBS News, *10:56:20 PM EDT, 7/20/69: The Historic Conquest of the Moon as Reported to the American People* (New York: Columbia Broadcasting System, 1970); Henry S.F. Cooper, *Apollo on the Moon* (New York: Dial Press, 1969); Tim Furniss, *"One Small Step"—The Apollo Missions, the Astronauts, the Aftermath: A Twenty Year Perspective* (Somerset, England: G.T. Foulis & Co., 1989); Richard S. Lewis, *Appointment on the Moon: The Inside Story of America's Space Adventure* (New York: Viking, 1969); John Noble Wilford, *We Reach the Moon: The New York Times Story of Man's Greatest Adventure* (New York: Bantam Books, 1969).

[87] On these missions see, W. David Compton, *Where No Man Has Gone Before: A History of Apollo Lunar Exploration Missions* (Washington, DC: NASA SP-4214, 1989); Stephen G. Brush, "A History of Modern Selenogony: Theoretical Origins of the Moon from Capture to Crash 1955-1984," *Space Science Reviews,* 47 (1988): 211-73; Stephen G. Brush, "Nickel for Your Thoughts: Urey and the Origin of the Moon," *Science,* 217 (3 September 1982): 891-98.

[88] United States Senate, Committee on Aeronautical and Space Sciences, *Apollo 13 Mission. Hearing, Ninety-first Congress, second session. April 24, 1970* (Washington, DC: Government Printing Office, 1970); United States Senate, Committee on Aeronautical and Space Sciences, *Apollo 13 Mission. Hearing, Ninety-first Congress, second session. June 30, 1970* (Washington, DC: Government Printing Office, 1970); Henry S.F. Cooper, Jr., *Thirteen: The Flight that Failed* (New York: Dial Press, 1973); "Four Days of Peril Between Earth and Moon: Apollo 13, Ill-Fated Odyssey," *Time,* 27 April 1970, pp. 14-18; "The Joyous Triumph of Apollo 13," *Life,* 24 April 1970, pp. 28-36; NASA Office of Public Affairs, *Apollo 13:* *"Houston, We've Got a Problem"* (Washington, DC: NASA EP-76, 1970).

[89] John Pike, "Apollo—Perspectives and Provocations," address to Cold War History Symposium, 11 May 1994, Ripley Center, Smithsonian Institution, Washington, DC.

[90] See Arnold S. Levine, *Managing NASA in the Apollo Era* (Washington, DC: NASA SP-4102, 1982); Sylvia D. Fries, *NASA Engineers and the Age of Apollo* (Washington, DC: NASA SP-4104, 1992); Sylvia K. Kraemer, "Organizing for Exploration."

[91] This seems to be a genuine strength of American engineering in general. See, Thomas P. Hughes, *American Genesis: A Century of Invention and Technological Enthusiasm* (New York: Viking, 1989).

[92] Quoted in Nicks, ed., *This Island Earth,* p. 3.

[93] Hall, "Project Apollo in Retrospect," pp. 25-26.

[94] As an example, see the argument made in George M. Low, Team Leader, to Mr. Richard Fairbanks, Director, Transition Resources and Development Group, "Report of the NASA Transition Team," 19 December 1980, NASA Historical Reference Collection, advocating strong presidential leadership to make everything right with the U.S. space program.

The Missions of Apollo

Dates: 1967-1972

Vehicles: *Saturn IB* and *Saturn V* launch vehicles
Apollo command/service module
Lunar module

Number of People Flown: 33

Highlights: First humans to leave Earth orbit
First human landing on the Moon

Apollo 7

October 11–22, 1968
Crew: Walter M. Schirra, Jr., Donn F. Eisele, Walter Cunningham

Apollo 7 was a confidence-builder. After the January 1967 *Apollo* launch pad fire, the *Apollo* command module had been extensively redesigned. Schirra, the only astronaut to fly *Mercury, Gemini* and *Apollo* missions, commanded this Earth-orbital shakedown of the command and service modules, With no lunar lander, *Apollo 7* was able to use the *Saturn IB* booster rather than the giant *Saturn V*. The *Apollo* hardware and all mission operations worked without any significant problems, and the Service Propulsion System (SPS)—the all-important engine that would place *Apollo* in and out of lunar orbit—made eight nearly perfect firings. Even though *Apollo's* larger cabin was more comfortable than *Gemini's,* eleven days in orbit took its toll on the astronauts. The food was bad, and all three developed colds. But their mission proved the spaceworthiness of the basic *Apollo* vehicle.

Apollo 8

December 21–27, 1968
Crew: Frank Borman, James A. Lovell, Jr., William A. Anders

The *Apollo 8* astronauts were the first human being to venture beyond low Earth orbit and visit another world. What was originally to have been an Earth-orbit checkout of the lunar lander became instead a race with the Soviets to become the first nation to orbit the Moon. The *Apollo 8* crew rode inside the command module, with no lunar lander attached. The were the first astronauts to be launched by the *Saturn V,* which had flown only twice before. The booster worked perfectly, as did the SPS engines that had been checked out on *Apollo 7*. *Apollo 8* entered lunar orbit on the morning of December 24, 1968. For the next 20 hours the astronauts circled the Moon, which appeared out their windows as a gray, battered wasteland. They took photographs, scouted future landing sites, and on Christmas Eve read from the Book of Genesis to TV viewers back on Earth. They also photographed the first Earthrise as seen from the Moon. *Apollo 8* proved the ability to navigate to and from the Moon, and gave a tremendous boost to the entire *Apollo* program.

Apollo 9

March 3–13, 1969
Crew: James A. McDivitt, David R. Scott, Russell L. Schweickart

Apollo 9 was the first space test of the third critical piece of *Apollo* hardware—the lunar module. For ten days, the astronauts put all three Apollo vehicles through their paces in Earth orbit, undocking and then redocking the lunar lander with the command module, just as they would in lunar orbit. For this and all subsequent *Apollo* flights, the crews were allowed to name their own spacecraft. The gangly lunar module was "Spider," the command module "Gumdrop," Schweickart and Scott performed a spacewalk, and Schweickart checked out the new *Apollo* spacesuit, the first to have its own life support system rather than being dependent on an umbilical connection to the spacecraft. *Apollo 9* gave proof that the *Apollo* machines were up to the task of orbital rendezvous and docking.

Apollo 10

May 18–26, 1969
Crew: Thomas P. Stafford, John W. Young, Eugene A. Ceman

This dress rehearsal for a Moon landing brought Stafford and Ceman's lunar module—nicknamed "Snoopy"—to within nine miles of the lunar surface, Except for that final stretch, the mission went exactly as a landing would have, both in space and on the ground, where *Apollo's* extensive tracking and control network was put through a dry run. Shortly after leaving low Earth orbit, the LM and the command service module separated, then redocked, top to top. Upon reaching lunar orbit, they separated again. While Young orbited the Moon alone in his command module "Charlie Brown," Stafford and Ceman checked out the LM's radar and ascent engine, rode out a momentary gyration in the lunar lander's motion (due to a faulty switch setting), and surveyed the *Apollo 11* landing site in the Sea of Tranquility . This test article of the lunar module was not equipped to land, however. *Apollo 10* also added another first—broadcasting live color TV from space.

Apollo 11

July 16–24, 1969
Crew: Neil A. Armstrong, Michael Collins, Edwin E. "Buzz" Aldrin, Jr.

Half of *Apollo's* primary goal—a safe return—was achieved at 4:17 p.m. Eastern Daylight Time on July 20, when Armstrong piloted "Eagle" to a touchdown on the Moon, with less than 30 seconds worth of fuel left in the lunar module. Six hours later, Armstrong took his famous "one giant leap for mankind." Aldrin joined him, and the two spent two-and-a-half hours drilling core samples, photographing what they saw and collecting rocks. After more than 21 hours on the lunar surface, they returned to Collins on board "Columbia," bringing 20.87 kilograms of lunar samples with them. The two Moon-walkers had left behind scientific instruments, an American flag and other mementos, including a plaque bearing the inscription: "Here Men From Planet Earth First Set Foot Upon the Moon. July 1969 A.D. We came in Peace For All Mankind."

Apollo 12

November 14–24, 1969
Crew: Charles "Pete" Conrad, Jr., Richard F. Gordon, Jr., Alan L. Bean

The second lunar landing was an exercise in precision targeting. The descent was automatic, with only a few manual corrections by Conrad. The landing, in the Ocean of Storms, brought the lunar module "Intrepid" within walking distance—182.88 meters—or a robot spacecraft that had touched down there two-and-a-half years earlier. Conrad and Bean brought pieces of the *Surveyor 3* back to Earth for analysis, and took two Moon-walks lasting just under four hours each. They collected rocks and set up experiments that measured the Moon's seismicity, solar wind flux and magnetic field. Meanwhile Gordon, on board the "Yankee Clipper" in lunar orbit, took multispectral photographs of the surface. The crew stayed an extra day in lunar orbit taking photographs. When "Intrepid's" ascent stage was dropped onto the Moon after Conrad and Bean rejoined Gordon in orbit, the seismometers the astronauts had left on the lunar surface registered the vibrations for more than an hour.

Apollo 13

April 11–17, 1970
Crew: James A. Lovell, Jr., Fred W. Haise, Jr., John L. Swigert, Jr.

The crew's understated radio message to Mission Control was "Okay, Houston, we've had a problem here." Within 321,860 kilometers of Earth, an oxygen tank in the service module exploded. The only solution was for the crew to abort their planned landing, swing around the Moon and return on a trajectory back to Earth. Since their command module "Odyssey" was almost completely dead, however, the three astronauts had to use the lunar module "Aquarius" as a crowded lifeboat for the return home. The four-day return trip was cold, uncomfortable and tense. But *Apollo 13* proved the program's ability to weather a major crisis and bring the crew back home safely.

Apollo 14

January 31–February 9, 1971
Crew: Alan B. Shepard, Jr., Stuart A. Roosa, Edgar D. Mitchell

After landing in the Fra Mauro region—the original destination for *Apollo 13*—Shepard and Mitchell took two Moon-walks, adding new seismic studies to the by-now familiar *Apollo* experiment package, and using a "lunar rickshaw" pull-cart to carry their equipment. A planned rock-collecting trip to the 1,000-foot-wide Cone Crater was dropped, however, when the astronauts had trouble finding their way around the lunar surface. Although later estimates showed that they had made it to within 30.48 meters of the crater's rim ,the explorer had become disoriented in the alien landscape. Roosa, meanwhile, took pictures from on board command module "Kitty Hawk" in lunar orbit. On the way back to Earth, the crew conducted the first U.S. materials processing experiments in space. The *Apollo 14* astronauts were the last lunar explorers to be quarantined on their return from the Moon.

Apollo 15

July 26–August 7, 1971
Crew: David R. Scott, James B. Irwin, Alfred M. Worden

The first of the longer, expedition-style lunar landing missions was also the first to include the lunar rover, a carlike vehicle that extended the astronauts' range. The lunar module *Falcon* touched down near the sinuous channel known as Hadley Rille, Scott and Irwin rode more than 27.36 kilometers in their rover, and had a free hand in their geological field studies compared to earlier astronauts. They brought back one of the prize trophies of the *Apollo* program—a sample of ancient lunar crust nicknamed the "Genesis Rock." *Apollo 15* also launched a small subsatellite for measuring particles and fields in the lunar vicinity. On the way back to Earth, Worden, who had flown solo on board *Endeavour* while his crewmates walked on the surface, conducted the first space-walk between Earth and the Moon to retrieve film from the side of the spacecraft.

Apollo 16

April 16–27, 1972
Crew: John W. Young, Thomas K. Mattingly II, Charles M. Duke, JR.

A malfunction in the main propulsion system of the lunar module "Orion" nearly caused their Moon landing to be scrubbed, but Young and Duke ultimately spent three days exploring the Descartes highland region, while Mattingly circled overhead in "Casper." What was thought to have been a region of volcanism turned out not to be, based on the astronauts' discoveries. Their collection of returned specimens included a 11.34 kilograms chunk that was the largest single rock returned by the *Apollo* astronauts. The *Apollo 16* astronauts also conducted performance tests with the lunar rover, at one time getting up to a top speed of 17.70 kilometers per hour.

Apollo 17

December 7-19, 1972
Crew: Eugene A. Cernan, Ronald E. Evans, Harrison H. "Jack" Schmitt

One of the last two men to set foot on the Moon was also the first scientist—astronaut/geologist Harrison Schmitt. While Evans circled in "America," Schmitt and Cernan collected a record 108.86 kilograms of rocks during three Moon-walks. The crew roamed for 33.80 kilometers through the Taurus-Littrow valley in their rover, discovered orange-colored soil, and left behind a plaque attached to their lander *Challenger*, which read: "Here Man completed his first exploration of the Moon, December 1972 A.D. May the spirit of peace in which we came be reflected in the lives of all mankind." The *Apollo* lunar program had ended.

Apollo Statistics

Spacecraft	Launch Date	Crew	Flight Time (days:hrs:min)	Highlights
Apollo 1	Jan. 27, 1967	Virgil I. Grissom Edward H. White II Roger Chafee		Planned as first manned Apollo Mission; fire during ground test on 1/27/67 took lives of astronauts; posthumously designated as *Apollo 1*.

There were no missions designated as Apollo 2 and Apollo 3.

Spacecraft	Launch Date	Crew	Flight Time (days:hrs:min)	Highlights
Apollo 4	Nov. 9, 1967	Unmanned	0:9:37	First flight of *Saturn V* launch vehicle. Placed unmanned Apollo command and service module in Earth orbit.
Apollo 5	Jan. 22, 1968	Unmanned	0:7:50	Earth orbital flight test of unmanned Lunar Module. Not recovered.
Apollo 6	April 4, 1968	Unmanned	0:9:57	Second unmanned test of *Saturn V* and Apollo.
Apollo 7	Oct. 11, 1968	Walter M. Schirra, Jr. Donn F. Eisele R. Walter Cunningham	10:20:9	First U.S. 3-person mission.
Apollo 8	Dec. 21, 1968	Frank Borman James A. Lovell, Jr. William A. Anders	6:3:1	First human orbit(s) of Moon; first human departure from Earth's sphere of influence; highest speed attained in human flight to date.
Apollo 9	Mar. 3, 1969	James A. McDivitt David R. Scott Russell L. Schweickart	10:1:1	Successfully simulated in Earth-orbit operation of lunar module to landing and takeoff from lunar surface and rejoining with command module.
Apollo 10	May 18, 1969	Thomas P. Stafford John W. Young Eugene A. Cernan	8:0:3	Successfully demonstrated complete system including lunar module to 14,300 m. from the lunar surface.
Apollo 11	July 16, 1969	Neil A. Armstrong Michael Collins Edwin E. Aldrin, Jr.	8:3:9	First human landing on lunar surface and safe return to Earth. First return of rock and soil samples to Earth, and human deployment of experiments on lunar surface.
Apollo 12	Nov. 14, 1969	Charles Conrad, Jr. Richard F. Gordon, Jr. Alan L. Bean	10:4:36	Second human lunar landing Explored surface of Moon and retrieved parts of *Surveyor 3* spacecraft, which landed in Ocean of Storms on Apr. 19, 1967.
Apollo 13	Apr. 11, 1970	James A. Lovell, Jr. Fred W. Haise, Jr. John L. Swigert, Jr.	5:22:55	Mission aborted; explosion in service module. Ship circled, Moon, with crew using LM as "lifeboat" until just before reentry.
Apollo 14	Jan. 31, 1971	Alan B. Shepard, Jr. Stuart A. Roosa Edgar D. Mitchell	9:0:2	Third human lunar landing. Mission demonstrated pinpoint landing capability and continued human exploration.
Apollo 15	July 26, 1971	David R. Scott Alfred M. Worden James B. Irwin	12:7:12	Fourth human lunar landing and first Apollo "J" series mission, which carried Lunar Roving Vehicle. Worden's inflight EVA of 38 min. 12 sec was performed during return trip.
Apollo 16	Apr. 16, 1972	John W. Young Charles M. Duke, Jr. Thomas K. Mattingly II	11:1:51	Fifth human lunar landing, with Lunar Roving Vehicle.
Apollo 17	Dec. 7, 1972	Eugene A. Cernan Harrison H. Schmitt Ronald E. Evans	12:13:52	Sixth and final Apollo human lunar landing, again with roving vehicle.

John F. Kennedy, Memorandum for Vice President, 20 April 1961, Presidential Files, John F. Kennedy Presidential Library, Boston, Massachusetts.

This memorandum led directly to the Apollo program. By posing the question "Is there any . . . space program which promises dramatic results in which we could win?" President Kennedy set in motion a review that concluded that only an effort to send Americans to the Moon met the criteria Kennedy had laid out. This memorandum followed a week of discussion within the White House on how best to respond to the challenge to U.S. interests posed by the 12 April 1961 orbital flight of Yuri Gagarin.

April 20, 1961

MEMORANDUM FOR

VICE PRESIDENT

In accordance with our conversation I would like
for you as Chairman of the Space Council to be in charge of
making an overall survey of where we stand in space.

1. Do we have a chance of beating the Soviets by
    putting a laboratory in space, or by a trip
    around the moon, or by a rocket to land on the
    moon, or by a rocket to go to the moon and
    back with a man. Is there any other space
    program which promises dramatic results in
    which we could win?

2. How much additional would it cost?

3. Are we working 24 hours a day on existing
    programs. If not, why not? If not, will you
    make recommendations to me as to how
    work can be speeded up.

4. In building large boosters should we put out
    emphasis on nuclear, chemical or liquid fuel,
    or a combination of these three?

5. Are we making maximum effort? Are we
    achieving necessary results?

I have asked Jim Webb, Dr. Weisner, Secretary
McNamara and other responsible officials to cooperate with
you fully. I would appreciate a report on this at the
earliest possible moment.

Lyndon B. Johnson, Vice President, Memorandum for the President, "Evaluation of Space Program," 28 April 1961, NASA Historical Reference Collection, NASA Headquarters, Washington, D.C.

This memorandum, prepared by Edward C. Welsh, Executive Secretary of the National Aeronautics and Space Council, and signed by Vice President Lyndon B. Johnson, was the first report to President Kennedy on the results of the review he had ordered on 20 April. The report identified a lunar landing by 1966 or 1967 as the first dramatic space project in which the United States could beat the Soviet Union. The Vice President identified "leadership" as the appropriate goal of U.S. efforts in space.

OFFICE OF THE VICE PRESIDENT

WASHINGTON, D. C.

April 28, 1961

MEMORANDUM FOR   PRESIDENT

Subject: Evaluation of Space Program.

Reference is to your April 20 memorandum asking certain questions
regarding this country's space program.

A detailed survey has not been completed in this time period. The
examination will continue. However, what we have obtained so far
from knowledgeable and responsible persons makes this summary
reply possible.

Among those who have participated in our deliberations have been the
Secretary and Deputy Secretary of Defense; General Schriever (AF);
Admiral Hayward (Navy); Dr. von Braun (NASA); the Administrator,
Deputy Administrator, and other top officials of NASA; the Special
Assistant to the President on Science and Technology; representatives
of the Director of the Bureau of the Budget; and three outstanding non-
Government citizens of the general public: Mr. George Brown
(Brown & Root, Houston, Texas); Mr. Donald Cook (American Electric
Power Service, New York, N. Y.); and Mr. Frank Stanton (Columbia
Broadcasting System, New York, N. Y.).

The following general conclusions can be reported:

> a. Largely due to their concentrated efforts and their
> earlier emphasis upon the development of large rocket
> engines, the Soviets are ahead of the United States in
> world prestige attained through impressive technological
> accomplishments in space.

> b. The U.S. has greater resources than the USSR for
> attaining space leadership but has failed to make the
> necessary hard decisions and to marshal those resources
> to achieve such leadership.

c. This country should be realistic and recognize that other nations, regardless of their appreciation of our idealistic values, will tend to align themselves with the country which they believe will be the world leader -- the winner in the long run. Dramatic accomplishments in space are being increasingly identified as a major indicator of world leadership.

d. The U.S. can, if it will, firm up its objectives and employ its resources with a reasonable chance of attaining world leadership in space during this decade. This will be difficult but can be made probable even recognizing the head start of the Soviets and the likelihood that they will continue to move forward with impressive successes. In certain areas, such as communications, navigation, weather, and mapping, the U.S. can and should exploit its existing advance position.

e. If we do not make the strong effort now, the time will soon be reached when the margin of control over space and over men's minds through space accomplishments will have swung so far on the Russian side that we will not be able to catch up, let alone assume leadership.

f. Even in those areas in which the Soviets already have the capability to be first and are likely to improve upon such capability, the United States should make aggressive efforts as the technological gains as well as the international rewards are essential steps in eventually gaining leadership. The danger of long lags or outright omissions by this country is substantial in view of the possibility of great technological breakthroughs obtained from space exploration.

g. Manned exploration of the moon, for example, is not only an achievement with great propaganda value, but it is essential as an objective whether or not we are first in its accomplishment -- and we may be able to be first. We cannot leapfrog such accomplishments, as they are essential sources of knowledge and experience for even greater successes in space. We cannot expect the Russians to transfer the benefits of their experiences or the advantages of their capabilities to us. We must do these things ourselves.

h. The American public should be given the facts as to how we stand in the space race, told of our determination to lead in that race, and advised of the importance of such leadership to our future.

i. More resources and more effort need to be put into our space program as soon as possible. We should move forward with a bold program, while at the same time taking every practical precaution for the safety of the persons actively participating in space flights.

* * * * * * *

As for the specific questions posed in your memorandum, the following brief answers develop from the studies made during the past few days. These conclusions are subject to expansion and more detailed examination as our survey continues.

Q.1 - Do we have a chance of beating the Soviets by putting a laboratory in space, or by a trip around the moon, or by a rocket to land on the moon, or by a rocket to go to the moon and back with a man. Is there any other space program which promises dramatic results in which we could win?

A.1 - The Soviets now have a rocket capability for putting a multi-manned laboratory into space and have already crash-landed a rocket on the moon. They also have the booster capability of making a soft landing on the moon with a payload of instruments, although we do not know how much preparation they have made for such a project. As for a manned trip around the moon or a safe landing and return by a man to the moon, neither the U.S. nor the USSR has such capability at this time, so far as we know. The Russians have had more experience with large boosters and with flights of dogs and man. Hence they might be conceded a time advantage in circumnavigation of the moon and also in a manned trip to the moon. However, with a strong effort, the United States could conceivably be first in those two accomplishments by 1966 or 1967.

There are a number of programs which the United States could pursue immediately and which promise significant world-wide advantage over the Soviets. Among these are communications satellites, meteorological and weather satellites, and navigation and mapping satellites. These are all areas in which we have already developed some competence. We have such programs and believe that the Soviets do not. Moreover, they are programs which could be made operational and effective within reasonably short periods of time and could, if properly programmed with the interests of other nations, make useful strides toward world leadership.

Q. 2 - How much additional would it cost?

A. 2 - To start upon an accelerated program with the afore-mentioned objectives clearly in mind, NASA has submitted an analysis indicating that about $500 million would be needed for FY 1962 over and above the amount currently requested of the Congress. A program based upon NASA's analysis would, over a ten-year period, average approximately $1 billion a year above the current estimates of the existing NASA program.

While the Department of Defense plans to make a more detailed submission to me within a few days, the Secretary has taken the position that there is a need for a strong effort to develop a large solid-propellant booster and that his Department is interested in undertaking such a project. It was understood that this would be programmed in accord with the existing arrangement for close cooperation with NASA, which Agency is undertaking some research in this field. He estimated they would need to employ approximately $50 million during FY 1962 for this work but that this could be financed through management of funds already requested in the FY 1962 budget. Future defense budgets would include requests for additional funding for this purpose; a preliminary estimate indicates that about $500 million would be needed in total.

Q. 3 - Are we working 24 hours a day on existing programs. If not, why not? If not, will you make recommendations to me as to how work can be speeded up.

A. 3 - There is not a 24-hour-a-day work schedule on existing NASA space programs except for selected areas in Project Mercury, the Saturn-C-1 booster, the Centaur engines and the final launching phases of most flight missions. They advise that their schedules have been geared to the availability of facilities and financial resources, and that hence their overtime and 3-shift arrangements exist only in those activities in which there are particular bottlenecks or which are holding up operations in other parts of the programs. For example, they have a 3-shift 7-day-week operation in certain work at Cape Canaveral; the contractor for Project Mercury has averaged a 54-hour week and employs two or three shifts in some areas; Saturn C-1 at Huntsville is working around the clock during critical test periods while the remaining work on this project averages a 47-hour week; the Centaur hydrogen engine is on a 3-shift basis in some portions of the contractor's plants.

This work can be speeded up through firm decisions to go ahead faster if accompanied by additional funds needed for the acceleration.

Q. 4 - In building large boosters should we put our emphasis on nuclear, chemical or liquid fuel, or a combination of these three?

A. 4 - It was the consensus that liquid, solid and nuclear boosters should all be accelerated. This conclusion is based not only upon the necessity for back-up methods, but also because of the advantages of the different types of boosters for different missions. A program of such emphasis would meet both so-called civilian needs and defense requirements.

Q. 5 - Are we making maximum effort? Are we achieving necessary results?

A. 5 - We are neither making maximum effort nor achieving results necessary if this country is to reach a position of leadership.

Lyndon B. Johnson

Wernher von Braun to the Vice President of the United States, 29 April 1961, NASA Historical Reference Collection, NASA Headquarters, Washington, D.C.

Of all those consulted during the presidentially-mandated space review, no one had been thinking longer about the future in space than Wernher von Braun. Even when he had led the development of the V-2 rocket for Germany during World War II, von Braun and his associates had been planning future space journeys. After coming to the United States after World War II, von Braun was a major contributor to popularizing the idea of human spaceflight. As he stressed in his letter, von Braun had been asked to participate in the review as an individual, not as the Director of NASA's Marshall Space Flight Center. Von Braun told the Vice President in his letter that the United States had "an excellent chance" of beating the Russians to a lunar landing.

April 29, 1961

The Vice President of the United States
The White House
Washington 25, D. C.

My dear Mr. Vice President:

This is an attempt to answer some of the questions about our national space program raised by The President in his memorandum to you dated April 20, 1961. I should like to emphasize that the following comments are strictly my own and do not necessarily reflect the official position of the National Aeronautics and Space Administration in which I have the honor to serve.

Question 1. Do we have a chance of beating the Soviets by putting a laboratory in space, or by a trip around the moon, or by a rocket to land on the moon, or by a rocket to go to the moon and back with a man? Is there any other space program which promises dramatic results in which we could win?

Answer: With their recent Venus shot, the Soviets demonstrated that they have a rocket at their disposal which can place 14,000 pounds of payload in orbit. When one considers that our own one-man Mercury space capsule weighs only 3900 pounds, it becomes readily apparent that the Soviet carrier rocket should be capable of

- launching several astronauts into orbit simultaneously. (Such an enlarged multi-man capsule could be considered and could serve as a small "laboratory in space".)

- soft-landing a substantial payload on the moon. My estimate of the maximum soft-landed net payload weight the Soviet rocket is capable of is about 1400 pounds (one-tenth of its low orbit payload). This weight capability is not sufficient to include a rocket for the return flight to earth of a man landed on the moon. But it is entirely adequate for a powerful radio transmitter which would relay lunar data back to earth and which would be abandoned on the lunar surface after completion of this

mission. A similar mission is planned for our
"Ranger" project, which uses an Atlas-Agena B
boost rocket. The "semi-hard" landed portion
of the Ranger package weighs 293 pounds.
Launching is scheduled for January 1962.

The existing Soviet rocket could furthermore hurl
a 4000 to 5000 pound capsule around the moon with ensuing re-entry
into the earth atmosphere. This weight allowance must be considered
marginal for a one-man round-the-moon voyage. Specifically, it
would not suffice to provide the capsule and its occupant with a "safe
abort and return" capability, - a feature which under NASA ground
rules for pilot safety is considered mandatory for all manned space
flight missions. One should not overlook the possibility, however,
that the Soviets may substantially facilitate their task by simply
waiving this requirement.

A rocket about ten times as powerful as the Soviet
Venus launch rocket is required to land a man on the moon and bring
him back to earth. Development of such a super rocket can be cir-
cumvented by orbital rendezvous and refueling of smaller rockets, but
the development of this technique by the Soviets would not be hidden
from our eyes and would undoubtedly require several years (possibly
as long or even longer than the development of a large direct-flight
super rocket).

Summing up, it is my belief that

a) we do not have a good chance of beating the Soviets
   to a manned "laboratory in space." The Russians
   could place it in orbit this year while we could
   establish a (somewhat heavier) laboratory only
   after the availability of a reliable Saturn C-1 which
   is in 1964.

b) we have a sporting chance of beating the Soviets to
   a soft-landing of a radio transmitter station on the
   moon. It is hard to say whether this objective is on
   their program, but as far as the launch rocket is
   concerned, they could do it at any time. We plan
   to do it with the Atlas-Agena B-boosted Ranger #3
   in early 1962.

c) we have a sporting chance of sending a 3-man crew around the moon ahead of the Soviets (1965/66). However, the Soviets could conduct a round-the-moon voyage earlier if they are ready to waive certain emergency safety features and limit the voyage to one man. My estimate is that they could perform this simplified task in 1962 or 1963.

d) we have an excellent chance of beating the Soviets to the first landing of a crew on the moon (including return capability, of course). The reason is that a performance jump by a factor 10 over their present rockets is necessary to accomplish this feat. While today we do not have such a rocket, it is unlikely that the Soviets have it. Therefore, we would not have to enter the race toward this obvious new goal in space exploration against hopeless odds favoring the Soviets. With an all-out crash program I think we could accomplish this objective in 1967/68.

Question 2. How much additional would it cost?

Answer: I think I should not attempt to answer this question before the exact objectives and the time plan for an accelerated United States space program have been determined. However, I can say with some degree of certainty that the necessary funding increase to meet objective d) above would be well over $1 Billion for FY 62, and that the required increases for subsequent fiscal years may run twice as high or more.

__Question 3.__   Are we working 24 hours a day on existing programs? If not, why not? If not, will you make recommendations to me as to how work can be speeded up.

__Answer:__   We are <u>not</u> working 24 hours a day on existing programs. At present, work on NASA's Saturn project proceeds on a basic one-shift basis, with overtime and multiple shift operations approved in critical "bottleneck" areas.

During the months of January, February and March 1961, NASA's George C. Marshall Space Flight Center, which has systems management for the entire Saturn vehicle and develops the large first stage as an inhouse project, has worked an average of 46 hours a week. This includes all administrative and clerical activities. In the areas critical for the Saturn project (design activities, assembly, inspecting, testing), average working time for the same period was 47.7 hours a week, with individual peaks up to 54 hours per week.

Experience indicates that in Research & Development work longer hours are not conducive to progress because of hazards introduced by fatigue. In the aforementioned critical areas, a second shift would greatly alleviate the tight scheduling situation. However, additional funds and personnel spaces are required to hire a second shift, and neither are available at this time. <u>In this area, help would be most effective.</u>

Introduction of a <u>third</u> shift <u>cannot</u> be recommended for Research & Development work. Industry-wide experience indicates that a two-shift operation with moderate but not excessive overtime produces the best results.

In industrial plants engaged in the Saturn program the situation is approximately the same. Moderately increased funding to permit greater use of premium paid overtime, prudently applied to real "bottleneck" areas, can definitely speed up the program.

Question 4.   In building large boosters should we put our emphasis on nuclear, chemical or liquid fuel, or a combination of those three?

Answer: It is the consensus of opinion among most rocket men and reactor experts that the future of the nuclear rocket lies in deep-space operations (upper stages of chemically-boosted rockets or nuclear space vehicles departing from an orbit around the earth) rather than in launchings (under nuclear power) from the ground. In addition, there can be little doubt that the basic technology of nuclear rockets is still in its early infancy. The nuclear rocket should therefore be looked upon as a promising means to extend and expand the scope of our space operations in the years beyond 1967 or 1968. It should not be considered as a serious contender in the big booster problem of 1961.

The foregoing comment refers to the simplest and most straightforward type of nuclear rocket, viz. the "heat transfer" or "blow-down" type, whereby liquid hydrogen is evaporated and superheated in a very hot nuclear reactor and subsequently expanded through a nozzle.

There is also a fundamentally different type of nuclear rocket propulsion system in the works which is usually referred to as "ion rocket" or "ion propulsion". Here, the nuclear energy is first converted into electrical power which is then used to expel "ionized" (i. e., electrically charged) particles into the vacuum of outer space at extremely high speeds. The resulting reaction force is the ion rocket's "thrust". It is in the very nature of nuclear ion propulsion systems that they cannot be used in the atmosphere. While very efficient in propellant economy, they are capable only of very small thrust forces. Therefore they do not qualify as "boosters" at all. The future of nuclear ion propulsion lies in its application for low-thrust, high-economy cruise power for interplanetary voyages.

As to "chemical or liquid fuel" The President's question undoubtedly refers to a comparison between "solid" and "liquid" rocket fuels, both of which involve chemical reactions.

At the present time, our most powerful rocket boosters (Atlas, first stage of Titan, first stage of Saturn) are all liquid fuel rockets and all available evidence indicates that the Soviets are also using liquid fuels for their ICBM's and space launchings. The largest solid fuel rockets in existence today (Nike Zeus booster, first stage Minuteman, first stage Polaris) are substantially smaller and less powerful. There is no question in my mind that, when it comes to building very powerful booster rocket systems, the body of experience available today with liquid fuel systems greatly exceeds that with solid fuel rockets.

There can be no question that larger and more powerful solid fuel rockets can be built and I do not believe that major breakthroughs are required to do so. On the other hand it should not be overlooked that a casing filled with solid propellant and a nozzle attached to it, while entirely capable of producing thrust, is not yet a rocket ship. And although the reliability record of solid fuel rocket <u>propulsion units</u>, thanks to their simplicity, is impressive and better than that of liquid propulsion units, this does not apply to <u>complete rocket systems</u>, including guidance systems, control elements, stage separation, etc.

Another important point is that booster performance should not be measured in terms of thrust force alone, but in terms of total impulse; i. e., the product of thrust force and operating time. For a number of reasons it is advantageous not to extend the burning time of solid fuel rockets beyond about 60 seconds, whereas most liquid fuel boosters have burning times of 120 seconds and more. Thus, a 3-million pound thrust solid rocket of 60 seconds burning time is actually not more powerful than a 1 1/2-million pound thrust liquid booster of 120 seconds burning time.

My recommendation is to substantially increase the level of effort and funding in the field of solid fuel rockets (by 30 or 50 million dollars for FY 62) with the immediate objectives of

- demonstration of the feasibility of very large segmented solid fuel rockets. (Handling and shipping of multi-million pound solid fuel rockets become unmanageable unless the rockets consist of smaller individual segments which can be assembled in building block fashion at the launching site.)

- development of simple inspection methods to make certain that such huge solid fuel rockets are free of dangerous cracks or voids

- determination of the most suitable operational methods to ship, handle, assemble, check and launch very large solid fuel rockets. This would involve a series of paper studies to answer questions such as

    a. Are clusters of smaller solid rockets, or huge, single poured-in-launch-site solid fuel rockets, possibly superior to segmented rockets? This question must be analyzed not just from the propulsion angle, but from the operational point of view for the total space transportation system and its attendant ground support equipment.

    b. Launch pad safety and range safety criteria (How is the total operation at Cape Canaveral affected by the presence of loaded multi-million pound solid fuel boosters?)

    c. Land vs off-shore vs sea launchings of large solid fuel rockets.

    d. Requirements for manned launchings (How to shut the booster off in case of trouble to permit safe mission abort and crew capsule recovery? If this is difficult, what other safety procedures should be provided?)

Question 5.   Are we making maximum effort?   Are we achieving necessary results?

Answer: No, I do not think we are making maximum effort.

In my opinion, the most effective steps to improve our national stature in the space field, and to speed things up would be to

- identify a few (the fewer the better) goals in our space program as objectives of highest national priority. (For example: Let's land a man on the moon in 1967 or 1968.)

- identify those elements of our present space program that would qualify as immediate contributions to this objective. (For example, soft landings of suitable instrumentation on the moon to determine the environmental conditions man will find there.)

- put all other elements of our national space program on the "back burner".

- add another more powerful *liquid fuel* booster to our national launch vehicle program. The design parameters of this booster should allow a certain flexibility for desired program re-orientation as more experience is gathered.

Example: Develop in addition to what is being done today, a first-stage *∧ liquid fuel* booster of twice the total impulse of Saturn's first stage, designed to be used in clusters if needed. With this booster we could

    a. double Saturn's presently envisioned payload. This additional payload capability would be very helpful for soft instrument landings on the moon, for circumlunar flights and for the final objective of a manned landing on the moon (if a few years from now the route via orbital re-fueling should turn out to be the more promising one.)

    b. assemble a much larger unit by strapping three or four boosters together into a cluster. This approach would be taken should, a few years hence, orbital rendezvous and refueling run into difficulties and the "direct route" for the manned lunar landing thus appears more promising.

Summing up, I should like to say that in the space race we are competing with a determined opponent whose peacetime economy is on a wartime footing. Most of our procedures are designed for orderly, peacetime conditions. I do not believe that we can win this race unless we take at least some measures which thus far have been considered acceptable only in times of a national emergency.

Yours respectfully,

/S/

Wernher von Braun

Overton Brooks to the Vice President of the United States, 4 May 1961, NASA Historical Reference Collection, NASA Headquarters, Washington, D.C.

Overton Brooks (D-LA), chair of the powerful House Committee on Science and Astronautics, wrote to Lyndon Johnson on 4 May proposing a strong U.S. civil program in space as the best means of demonstrating "<u>unequivocal leadership in Space Exploration</u>." He emphasized the prestige factors involved in the U.S./U.S.S.R. rivalry during the Cold War, and offered several possible options to pursue in meeting the challenge, among them an aggressive Apollo effort.

COMMITTEE ON SCIENCE AND ASTRONAUTICS

HOUSE OF REPRESENTATIVES

WASHINGTON, D.C.

May 4, 1961

MEMORANDUM

To: The Honorable Lyndon B. Johnson, Chairman,
National Aeronautics and Space Council

From: Overton Brooks, Chairman,
House Committee on Science and Astronautics

Subject: Recommendations re the National Space Program

General

It is my belief -- and I think on this point that I can speak for our committee -- that the United States must do whatever is necessary to gain unequivocal leadership in Space Exploration.

This means the procurement and utilization of sufficient scientific talent, labor and material resources as well as the expenditure of sufficient funds. This means working around the clock, if need be, in all areas of our Space program -- not just a few.

The reason is patent. Rightly or wrongly, leadership in space research and exploration has assumed such a powerful position among the elements which form the political stature of our country in the eyes of the world that we cannot afford to slight it in any fashion whatsoever. This is perhaps even more true of the non-military phase of our national space endeavor than it is of the military. Obviously, neither phase can be slighted.

According to the best information and estimates available to our committee, the Soviets are putting about 2%

of their gross national product into their space effort --
possibly as much as 2½%. For various reasons, this is a
difficult thing to correlate in terms of equivalent dollars.
But I think it is indicative of national attitudes and effort
to contrast the Russian percentage with the less than one-
half of one per cent of the United States gross national product
which is going into the space program, civilian and military.
A similar financial commitment on our part would involve some
$10 billion a year.

Of course, I am not suggesting anything of this
magnitude, but I do believe we need to accelerate our space
program to the maximum that it can be accelerated by adding
money to it.

I understand the restrictions and limitations im-
posed by our budget and by the many other legitimate demands
for federal money. But I also am convinced that this space
effort must be made and can be made within the flexible confines of the existing budget.

Let me emphasize that while the recommendations to
follow deal mainly with the augmentation of our immediate
and short-range program, we on this committee are equally
committed to a forceful and stepped-up long-range endeavor.
We believe that a particular effort must be made to strengthen
such programs as Apollo, Saturn, Rover and the solid-segmented
and F-1 liquid engine concepts.

I totally reject the defeatist notion that we are
so far behind the Soviets in certain space areas that there
is little point in trying to overtake them, nor can I accept
the philosophy that our Space endeavor should be limited to
a moderately-paced, purely scientific program. In today's
volatile world our very security is linked to a dynamic,
operational, broad-gauged program.

WHAT THE UNITED STATES CAN DO ON A SHORT-TERM BASIS TO RAISE U. S. PRESTIGE WITH RESPECT TO PRACTICAL SPACE ACCOMPLISHMENTS

1. There is no doubt that it will be five to eight years before we can overtake the Soviets with respect to operational use of very large rockets of either the nuclear or chemical variety.

2. If we are to do anything in the immediate future to regain prestige, we are intimately tied to the propulsion system now in being. This is basically Atlas, Titan and Thor. Don't expect too much use out of Saturn until 1965.

3. Based on Atlas, Titan, and Thor, our only hope for short-term payoff will be to accelerate the operational use of what I consider the utility packages. These are:
    (a) Worldwide communications satellites
    (b) Worldwide television satellites
    (c) Worldwide weather satellites
    (d) Worldwide navigation satellites

4. <u>Worldwide communications and television satellites</u>

I believe that we can have them as useful systems in three years on an experimental basis. They are important because <u>the nation that controls worldwide communications and television will ultimately have that nation's language become the universal tongue.</u>

5. <u>Worldwide weather satellite systems</u>

We have already developed a strong and sound technological leadership in this area. It appears that we excel the Soviets in the development of this type of satellite. This is one area where we can win worldwide competitive support. The world could be offered a limited operational system within one year, and a completely operational system within three years if we put the money behind it. Attendant political, psychological, and economic benefits that would accrue can be easily measured against our political goals.

6. The navigation satellite

The Transit satellite is well on its way to being operational. Within one year you could achieve a demonstrable worldwide navigation system. Within three years you could have a fully operational system, including the development of ground read-out equipment which would be relatively inexpensive and could be offered to all countries of the world. Such ground read-out equipment is already under development. Offering all nations of the world the use of this satellite will have an important effect with respect to the image we desire to project internationally.

7. Funding of utility packages

My staff has estimated that it would require an additional $100 to $150 million to accelerate the programs mentioned above to insure having them all operational within three years, except for the television relay satellite, which may only be operational on an experimental basis within that time. The significant reason for increased funds will not be the cost of payload development, but rather the procurement of launch vehicles, launching services, and the production of worldwide read-out equipment.

8. Inflatable structures

Current developments in inflatable structures may be significant, in that they represent one of the few ways in a relatively short time span of placing large structures in space with our current rocket vehicles. Inflatable structures make small packages in the nose of a rocket and in space can be inflated to large, complex shapes with plastic foam hardened in double walls to create light weight, rigid structures. They could be useful for placing payloads into space which we have previously thought could not be done until we had the Saturn operational. Perhaps $6 to $8 million invested in this development area might have significant short-term payoff.

A POSSIBLE, SHORT-TERM DRAMATIC ACHIEVEMENT WITH RESPECT TO BASIC SCIENCE

THE ORBITING ASTRONOMICAL OBSERVATORY

The first nation which is able, on the basis of observation, to make a cosmological determination of the origin, evolution and nature of the universe will have reached one of the great milestones in the history of man.

Not only will this determination be a scientific achievement of the first magnitude, but it very likely will have a highly dramatic impact on the populations of every nation. All people are instinctively and deeply interested in how the world began and where it is going.

Such a determination can also be expected to capture the fascinated attention of every physical scientist -- men and women who have been trying for years to learn the truth concerning the creation of the universe and who are divided over the conflicting Explosion, Steady-State and Expansion-Contraction theories of leading cosmologists.

Astronomers agree that the only way to make such a determination is through observation. They also agree that perhaps the largest remaining obstacle to the necessary observation is acquiring the capability to observe from a point undisturbed by the earth's atmosphere.

This is what the 3500-pound, unmanned Orbiting Astronomical Observatory (OAO) is designed to do.

This is also a portion of our scientific satellite program which is being funded on a relative shoestring and without any particular urgency attached to it.

In view of the potential drama and prestige connected with the OAO, and in view of the fact that it does not require excessive developmental time, it is suggested that this program be provided with additional funds and assigned a high priority.

The OAO is not dependent on undeveloped boosters. It contemplates use of the Atlas-Agena B, which is in existence. The planned payload for the first OAO, while complicated, presents no exceptionally difficult problems. The most difficult problem connected with the OAO appears to be the very high order of stabilization necessary to permit an accurate charting of the heavens -- but here again the basic techniques are known. It is a matter of development.

NASA, in its 1962 recommendations, is asking about $5.7 million for further development of the payload and $12 million for launch and flight units. A request to the Budget Bureau for an additional $7 million for this program was not approved, which will slow even the present schedule.

The first OAO is not scheduled for launch until late 1963. Indications are, however, that the program can be speeded up considerably with the addition of not more than $15 or $20 million and with the assignment of priority to it.

It is therefore recommended that:

(1) The OAO be assigned all necessary funding and priority to get it off the ground at the earliest possible moment. This should include adequate backups both for launch vehicles and for a variety of payloads.

(2) An ad hoc Cosmology Assessment Board composed of about five noted astronomers (such as Whipple of Smithsonian, Gold of Cornell, Code of Wisconsin, Roman of NASA, Mayall of Kitts Peak) be formed to work out the details of the experiments -- and to evaluate subsequent results.

(3) The emphasis on this program not be publicized until the Board is ready to release data which has significant cosmological meaning.

It is recognized that important findings in this field will take time and study and that they will not immediately be conclusive. Nonetheless it is believed that results which may even _point_ in the direction of the truth concerning the nature of the universe may carry an impact to make our scientific findings to date pale by comparison. We should not let Russia report the first important findings in this field.

To get moving on this program we need not wait for the development of a Saturn, a nuclear rocket or a life support system. We can begin now and cheaply.

WHAT THE UNITED STATES CAN DO ON AN INTERMEDIATE-TERM BASIS TO GAIN AND MAINTAIN WORLD LEADERSHIP IN SPACE TECHNOLOGY

1. We should embark immediately upon a back-up or alternate for the Saturn project. All indications are that Saturn will slip.

2. Industry, through NASA or DOD, or both, should be given an immediate go-ahead in the development of large, segmented, clusterable solid rocket engines to back up the Saturn.

3. A family of large, first stage "space trucks" should be developed so that proper upper-stage rocket vehicles and our payload program can be effectively planned and designed.

4. The Rover Project should be pursued vigorously; however, since this is one area where we may leapfrog the Soviets, we need insurance. We should immediately embark upon a back-up nuclear rocket development, should Rover fail to be the correct approach. There is a great deal of reactor "know-how" and rocket engine "know-how", which I do not believe is being utilized to the fullest in achieving a successful nuclear rocket. We may be overlooking many bright ideas by giving the Rover Project group monopoly on the development of nuclear rockets.

5. There is need for sustained development in the chemical rocket field, despite the anticipated successful development of nuclear rocket engines. Both liquid and solid rocket developments must continue at high priority, since there is a place for both the chemical and nuclear boosters in the national program.

6. It is important that military designed criteria be incorporated in NASA-developed large space trucks, because I do not think we can afford to have two agencies running parallel programs which will spend many billions of dollars over the next ten to fifteen years.

7. Because large space boosters are so expensive, serious thought should be given to designing both manned and unmanned recoverable systems.

8. If we accelerate our space program, we will soon exhaust our storehouse of basic and applied research. We must put more emphasis in these areas by drawing in more scientific talent and channeling more funds into the fundamentals of basic space technology.

9. We should pursue vigorously our man-in-space program. We cannot concede the Moon to the Soviets, for it is conceivable that the nation which controls the Moon may well control the Earth.

10. The military aspects of space must not be over-looked. We should embark upon serious developments in the area of anti-satellite weapons, covert reconnaissance, and other offensive and defensive systems which can be done better from a space environment than an earth environment. These developments admittedly will be expensive, therefore we must be careful that we do not embark upon military space systems for the pure sake of doing them from space if they can be done more effectively and economically from Earth.

11. We must start now to plan not only the exploration of the Moon, but the exploration of the planets if we are to wrest the initiative in this area from the Soviets. The driving force which has brought man to the level of mastery of the world around him has been his insatiable intellectual curiosity. I believe we are in the initial phase of man's drive to break out into the universe.

12. Can we support a broad-based national space program? I have already said that the United States can sustain a massive space effort, and if carefully planned, it can be accomplished without creating undue imbalance in our structure for scientific research and in our economy. A $5 billion a year space program represents only about 1% of our gross national product, even half of which offers returns crucial to the leadership, the prestige, and perhaps even the survival of the United States.

QUESTIONS WHICH I BELIEVE SHOULD BE CONSIDERED BY THE SPACE
COUNCIL

1. Has there been developed a recognizable set of
national space objectives?

2. Are we merely reacting to Soviet accomplishments
with space projects that parallel theirs? If so, we can never
hope to surpass them because we will always be behind.

3. Will the Space Council staff, as now envisioned,
be capable of providing the information the Council will need
make decisions on a national basis? Will the Council insure
that its staff is made up of knowledgeable civilians, rather
than utilizing military personnel?

4. Will the Space Council review both DOD and NASA
programs, assess them against the national objectives, limit
overlap and duplication, and set plateaus of achievement?

5. Will the Space Council have as its principal
objective the tying together of our technological goals in
space with our geopolitical goals?

6. Does the Space Council intend to fix program
responsibilities and write report cards?

7. Will the members of the Space Council continue
to work closely with the Committees in Congress charged with
the legislative responsibility for the national space effort?

8. Will the Space Council adjudicate DOD-NASA
conflict?

9. Since the DOD and NASA members of the Space
Council have an understandable stake in the competition for
dollars channeled into the national space program, will it
be possible to make realistic program determinations between
the two without independent staff studies by competent experts not connected with either DOD or NASA?

10. Will the Council be sufficiently staffed to develop a national 5, 10, 15, 20 - year program for space endeavor which takes into consideration not only our technological goals in space, but the international political goals of the United States?

John F. Kennedy, Excerpts from "Urgent National Needs" speech to a Joint Session of Congress, 25 May 1961, Presidential Files, John F. Kennedy Library, Boston, Massachusetts.

This is the section of President Kennedy's "reading text" of his address to a Joint Session of Congress in which he called for sending Americans to the Moon "before this decade is out." President Kennedy in his own hand modified the prepared text of his remarks. The text as written, modified, and ultimately delivered vary considerably. Kennedy also ad-libbed three additional paragraphs near the end of his speech.

To this end I soon shall send to the
Congress a measure to establish a
strengthened and enlarged Disarmament
Administration. Such an agency can
intensify and improve our studies and
research on this problem, looking
forward to the day when reason will
prevail, and all nations of the world
will be prepared to accept a realistic
and safeguarded disarmament in a world
of law.

IX. Space

Finally, if we are to win the
battle for men's minds,

the dramatic achievements in space
which occurred in recent weeks should
have made clear to us all the impact
of this new frontier of human
adventure. Since early in my term,
our efforts in space have been under
review. With the advice of the
Vice President we have examined where
we are strong and where we are not,
where we may succeed and where we may
not. Now it is time to take longer
strides -- time for a great new
American enterprise -- time for this
nation to take a clearly leading role
in space achievement, *which in many ways*
may hold the key to our future on earth.

I believe we possess all the
resources and all the talents
necessary. But the facts of the
matter are that we have never made
the national decisions or marshalled
the national resources required for
such leadership. We have never
specified long-range goals on an
urgent time schedule, or managed our
resources and our time so as to insure
their fulfillment.

Recognizing the head start
obtained by the Soviets with their
large rocket engines, which gives
them many months of lead-time,

and recognizing the likelihood that
they will exploit this lead for some
time to come in still more impressive
successes, we nevertheless are
required to make new efforts. For
while we cannot guarantee that we
shall one day be first, we can
guarantee that any failure to make
this effort will find us last. We
take an additional risk by making it
in full view of the world -- but as
shown by the feat of astronaut Shepard,
this very risk enhances our stature
when we are successful. But this is
not merely a race.

Space is open to us now; and our
eagerness to share its meaning is not
governed by the efforts of others. We
go into space because whatever mankind
must undertake, _free_ men must fully
share.

I therefore ask the Congress,
above and beyond the increases I have
earlier requested for space activities,
to provide the funds which are needed
to meet the following national goals:

First, I believe that this nation
should commit itself to achieving the
goal, before this decade is out,
of landing a man on the moon and
returning him safely to earth.

No single space project in this period
will be more ~~exciting, or~~ more
impressive, or more important for the
long-range exploration of space; and
none will be so difficult or expensive
to accomplish. Including necessary
~~supporting research,~~ this objective
will require an additional $531 million
this year and still higher sums in the
future. We propose to accelerate
development of the appropriate lunar
space craft. We propose to develop
alternate liquid and solid fuel
boosters of much larger than any now
being developed, until certain which
is superior.

We propose additional funds for
other engine development and for
unmanned explorations -- explorations
which are particularly important for
one purpose which this nation will
never overlook: the survival of the
man who first makes this daring flight.
But in a very real sense, it will not
be one man going to the moon -- it will
be an entire nation. For all of us
must work to put him there.

Second, an additional $23 million,
together with $7 million already
available, will accelerate development
of the ROVER nuclear rocket.

This ~~is a technological enterprise~~ in
~~which we are well on the way to
striking progress, and which~~ gives
promise of some day providing a means
for even more exciting and ambitious
exploration of space, perhaps beyond
the moon, perhaps to the very ends of
the solar system itself.

Third, an additional $50 million
will make the most of our present
leadership by accelerating the use of
space satellites for world-wide
communications. When we have put into
space a system that will enable people
in remote areas of the earth to
exchange messages, hold conversations,

and eventually see television programs,
we will have achieved a success as
beneficial as it will be striking.

Fourth, an additional $75
million -- of which $53 million is for
the Weather Bureau -- will help give us
at the earliest possible time a satellite system for world-wide weather
observation. Such a system will be of
inestimable commercial and scientific
value; and the information it provides
will be made freely available to all
the nations of the world.

Let it be clear that I am asking
the Congress and the country to accept
a firm commitment to a new course of
action --

a course which will last for many
years and carry very heavy costs --
an estimated $7-9 billion additional
over the next five years. If we were
to go only halfway, or reduce our
sights in the face of difficulty, it
would be better not to go at all.

Let me stress also that more
money alone will not do the job.
This decision demands a major national
commitment of scientific and technical
manpower, material and facilities,
and the possibility of their diversion
from other important activities where
they are already thinly spread. It
means a degree of dedication,

organization and discipline which have
not always characterized our research
and development efforts. It means we
cannot afford undue work stoppages,
inflated costs of material or talent,
wasteful interagency rivalries, or a
high turnover of key personnel.

New objectives and new money
cannot solve these problems. They
could, in fact, aggravate them
further -- unless every scientist,
every engineer, every serviceman,
every technician, contractor, and
civil servant involved gives his
personal pledge that this nation will
move forward, with the full speed of
freedom, in the exciting adventure of
space.

"Concluding Remarks by Dr. Wernher von Braun about Mode Selection for the Lunar Landing Program," 7 June 1962, Lunar-Orbit Rendezvous File, NASA Historical Reference Collection, NASA Headquarters, Washington, D.C.

At the conclusion of an all-day meeting of key NASA personnel over the method of reaching the Moon on 7 June 1962, Wernher von Braun, director of the Marshall Space Flight Center and one of the most important proponents of the "Earth-Orbit Rendezvous" mode, acquiesced his position in favor of a "Lunar-Orbit Rendezvous" concept. His reasons for doing so are presented in this text of his remarks at the meeting. The mode decision allowed the Apollo program to move forward to final hardware design, a critical component in von Braun's acquiescence in the "Lunar-Orbit Rendezvous" concept for without it meeting the Kennedy mandate to land on the Moon before the end of the decade might have been unrealizable.

CONCLUDING REMARKS BY DR. WERNHER VON BRAUN
ABOUT MODE SELECTION FOR THE LUNAR LANDING PROGRAM
GIVEN TO DR. JOSEPH F. SHEA, DEPUTY DIRECTOR (SYSTEMS)
OFFICE OF MANNED SPACE FLIGHT
JUNE 7, 1962

In the previous six hours we presented to you the results of some
of the many studies we at Marshall have prepared in connection with
the Manned Lunar Landing Project. The purpose of all these studies
was to identify potential technical problem areas, and to make sound
and realistic scheduling estimates. All studies were aimed at assisting
you in your final recommendation with respect to the mode to be chosen
for the Manned Lunar Landing Project.

Our general conclusion is that all four modes investigated are
technically feasible and could be implemented with enough time and
money. We have, however, arrived at a definite list of preferences
in the following order:

1. Lunar Orbit Rendezvous Mode - with the strong
   recommendation (to make up for the limited
   growth potential of this mode) to initiate, simultaneously, the development of an unmanned, fully
   automatic, one-way C-5 logistics vehicle.

2. Earth Orbit Rendezvous Mode (Tanking Mode).

3. C-5 Direct Mode with minimum size Command
   Module and High Energy Return.

4. Nova or C-8 Mode.

I shall give you the reasons behind this conclusion in just one minute.

But first I would like to reiterate once more that <u>it is absolutely
mandatory that we arrive at a definite mode decision within the next few
weeks, preferably by the first of July, 1962.</u> We are already losing time
in our over-all program as a result of a lacking mode decision.

A typical example is the S-IVB contract. If the S-IVB stage is to serve not only as the third (escape) stage for the C-5, but also as the second stage for the C-1B needed in support of rendezvous tests, a flyable S-IVB will be needed at least one year earlier than if there was no C-1B at all. The impact of this question on facility planning, build-up of contractor level of effort, etc., should be obvious.

Furthermore, if we do not freeze the mode now, we cannot lay out a definite program with a schedule on which the budgets for FY-1964 and following can be based. Finally, if we do not make a clear-cut decision on the mode very soon, our chances of accomplishing the first lunar expedition in this decade will fade away rapidly.

I. WHY DO WE RECOMMEND LUNAR ORBIT RENDEZVOUS MODE PLUS C-5 ONE-WAY LOGISTICS VEHICLE?

  a. We believe this program offers the highest confidence factor of successful accomplishment within this decade.

  b. It offers an adequate performance margin. With storable propellants, both for the Service Module and Lunar Excursion Module, we should have a comfortable padding with respect to propulsion performance and weights. The performance margin could be further increased by initiation of a back-up development aimed at a High Energy Propulsion System for the Service Module and possibly the Lunar Excursion Module. Additional performance gains could be obtained if current proposals by Rocketdyne to increase the thrust and/or specific impulses of the F-1 and J-2 engines were implemented.

  c. We agree with the Manned Spacecraft Center that the designs of a maneuverable hyperbolic re-entry vehicle and of a lunar landing vehicle constitute the two most critical tasks in producing a successful lunar spacecraft. A drastic separation of these two functions into two separate elements is bound to greatly simplify the development of the spacecraft system. Developmental cross-feed between results from simulated or actual landing tests, on the one hand, and re-entry tests, on the other, are minimized if no attempt is made to include the Command Module into the lunar landing process. The mechanical separation of the two functions would virtually permit completely parallel developments of the Command Module and the Lunar Excursion Module. While it may be difficult to accurately appraise this advantage in terms of months to be gained, we have no doubt whatsoever that such a procedure will indeed result in very substantial saving of time.

d. We believe that the combination of the Lunar Orbit Rendezvous Mode and a C-5 one-way Logistics Vehicle offers a great growth potential. After the first successful landing on the moon, demands for follow-on programs will essentially center on increased lunar surface mobility and increased material supplies for shelter, food, oxygen, scientific instrumentation, etc. It appears that the Lunar Excursion Module, when refilled with propellants brought down by the Logistics Vehicle, constitutes an ideal means for lunar surface transportation. First estimates indicate that in the 1/6 G gravitational field of the moon, the Lunar Excursion Module, when used as a lunar taxi, would have a radius of action of at least 40 miles from around the landing point of the Logistics Vehicle. It may well be that on the rocky and treacherous lunar terrain the Lunar Excursion Module will turn out to be a far more attractive type of a taxi than a wheeled or caterpillar vehicle.

e. We believe the Lunar Orbit Rendezvous Mode using a single C-5 offers a very good chance of ultimately growing into a C-5 direct capability. At this time we recommend against relying on the C-5 Direct Mode because of its need for a much lighter command module as well as a high energy landing and return propulsion system. While it may be unwise to count on the availability of such advanced equipment during this decade (this is why this mode was given a number 3 rating) it appears entirely within reach in the long haul.

f. If and when at some later time a reliable nuclear third stage for Saturn C-5 emerges from the RIFT program, the performance margin for the C-5 Direct Mode will become quite comfortable.

g. Conversely, if the Advanced Saturn C-5 were dropped in favor of a Nova or C-8, it would completely upset all present plans for the implementation of the RIFT program. Contracts, both for the engines and the RIFT stage, have already been let and would probably have to be cancelled until a new program could be developed.

h. We conclude from our studies that an automatic pinpoint letdown on the lunar surface going through a circumlunar orbit and using a landing beacon is entirely possible. Whether this method should be limited to the C-5 Logistics Vehicle or be adopted as a secondary mode for the Lunar Excursion Module is a matter that should be carefully discussed with the Manned Spacecraft Center. It may well be that the demand for incorporation of an additional automatic landing capability in the Lunar Excursion Module buys more trouble than gains.

i.   The Lunar Orbit Rendezvous Mode augmented by a C-5 Logistics Vehicle undoubtedly offers the cleanest managerial interfaces between the Manned Spacecraft Center, Marshall Space Flight Center, Launch Operations Center and all our contractors.   While the precise effect of this may be hard to appraise, it is a commonly accepted fact that the number and the nature of technical and managerial interfaces are very major factors in conducting a complex program on a tight time schedule.   There are already a frightening number of interfaces in existence in our Manned Lunar Landing Program.   There are interfaces between the stages of the launch vehicles, between launch vehicles and spacecraft, between complete space vehicles and their ground equipment, between manned and automatic checkout, and in the managerial area between the Centers, the Washington Program Office, and the contractors.   The plain result of too many interfaces is a continuous and disastrous erosion of the authority vested in the line organization and the need for more coordination meetings, integration groups, working panels, ad-hoc committees, etc.   Every effort should therefore be made to reduce the number of technical and managerial interfaces to a bare minimum.

j.   Compared with the C-5 Direct Mode or the Nova/C-8 Mode, the Lunar Orbit Rendezvous Mode offers the advantage that no existing contracts for stages (if we go to Nova) or spacecraft systems (if we go to C-5 Direct) have to be terminated; that the contractor structure in existence can be retained; that the contract negotiations presently going on can be finished under the existing set of ground rules; that the contractor build-up program (already in full swing) can be continued as planned; that facilities already authorized and under construction can be built as planned, etc.

k.   We at the Marshall Space Flight Center readily admit that when first exposed to the proposal of the Lunar Orbit Rendezvous Mode we were a bit skeptical - particularly of the aspect of having the astronauts execute a complicated rendezvous maneuver at a distance of 240,000 miles from the earth where any rescue possibility appeared remote.   In the meantime, however, we have spent a great deal of time and effort studying the four modes, and we have come to the conclusion that this particular disadvantage is far outweighed by the advantages listed above.

We understand that the Manned Spacecraft Center was also quite skeptical at first when John Houbolt of Langley advanced the proposal of the Lunar Orbit Rendezvous Mode, and that it took them quite a while to substantiate the feasibility of the method and finally endorse it.

Against this background it can, therefore, be concluded that the issue of "invented here" versus "not invented here" does not apply to either the Manned Spacecraft Center or the Marshall Space Flight Center; that both Centers have actually embraced a scheme suggested by a third source. Undoubtedly, personnel of MSC and MSFC have by now conducted more detailed studies on all aspects of the four modes than any other group. Moreover, it is these two Centers to which the Office of Manned Space Flight would ultimately have to look to "deliver the goods". I consider it fortunate indeed for the Manned Lunar Landing Program that both Centers, after much soul searching, have come to identical conclusions. This should give the Office of Manned Space Flight some additional assurance that our recommendations should not be too far from the truth.

II. WHY DO WE NOT RECOMMEND THE EARTH ORBIT RENDEZVOUS MODE?

Let me point out again that we at the Marshall Space Flight Center consider the Earth Orbit Rendezvous Mode entirely feasible. Specifically, we found the Tanking Mode substantially superior to the Connecting Mode. Compared to the Lunar Orbit Rendezvous Mode, it even seems to offer a somewhat greater performance margin. This is true even if only the nominal two C-5's (tanker and manned lunar vehicle) are involved, but the performance margin could be further enlarged almost indefinitely by the use of additional tankers.

We have spent more time and effort here at Marshall on studies of the Earth Orbit Rendezvous Mode (Tanking and Connecting Modes) than on any other mode. This is attested to by six big volumes describing all aspects of this mode. Nor do we think that in the light of our final recommendation - to adopt the Lunar Orbit Rendezvous Mode instead - this effort was in vain. Earth Orbit Rendezvous as a general operational procedure will undoubtedly play a major role in our over-all national space flight program, and the use of it is even mandatory in developing a Lunar Orbit Rendezvous capability.

The reasons why, in spite of these advantages, we moved it down to position number 2 on our totem pole are as follows:

a. We consider the Earth Orbit Rendezvous Mode more complex and costlier than Lunar Orbit Rendezvous. Moreover, lunar mission success with Earth Orbit Rendezvous requires two consecutive successful launches. If, for example, after a successful tanker launch, the manned lunar vehicle aborts during its ascent, or fails to get off the pad within a certain permissible period of time, the first (tanker) flight must also be written off as useless for the mission.

b. The interface problems arising between the Manned Spacecraft Center and the Marshall Space Flight Center, both in the technical and management areas, would be more difficult if the Earth Orbit Rendezvous Mode was adopted. For example, if the tanker as an unmanned vehicle was handled by MSFC, and the flight of the manned lunar vehicle was conducted by the Manned Spacecraft Center, a managerial interface arises between target and chaser. On the other hand, if any one of the two Centers would take over the entire mission, it would probably bite off more than it could chew, with the result of even more difficult and unpleasant interface problems.

     c. According to repeated statements by Bob Gilruth, the Apollo Command Module in its presently envisioned form is simply unsuited for lunar landing because of the poor visibility conditions and the undesirable supine position of the astronauts during landing.

III. WHY DO WE NOT RECOMMEND THE C-5 DIRECT MODE?

     It is our conviction that the C-5 Direct Mode will ultimately become feasible - once we know more about hyperbolic re-entry, and once we have adequate high energy propulsion systems available that can be used conveniently and reliably on the surface of the moon. With the advent of a nuclear third stage for C-5, the margin for this capability will be substantially widened, of course.

     a. Our main reason against recommending the C-5 Direct Mode is its marginal weight allowance for the spacecraft and the demand for high energy return propulsion, combined with the time factor, all of which would impose a very substantial additional burden on the Manned Spacecraft Center.

     b. The Manned Spacecraft Center has spent a great deal of time and effort in determining realistic spacecraft weights. In the opinion of Bob Gilruth and Chuck Mathews, it would simply not be realistic to expect that a lunar spacecraft light enough to be used with the C-5 Direct Mode could be developed during this decade with an adequate degree of confidence.

     c. The demand for a high energy return propulsion system, which is implicit in the C-5 Direct Mode, is considered undesirable by the Manned Spacecraft Center - at the present state-of-the-art at least - because this propulsion system must also double up as an extra-atmospheric abort propulsion system. For this purpose, MSC considers a propulsion system as simple and reliable as possible (storable and hypergolic propellants) as absolutely mandatory. We think the question of inherent reliability of storable versus high energy propulsion systems - and their usability in the lunar surface environment - can be argued, but as long as the requirement for "storables" stands, the C-5 Direct Mode is not feasible performance-wise.

d. NASA has already been saddled with one program (Centaur) where the margin between performance claims for launch vehicle and demands for payload weights were drawn too closely. We do not consider it prudent to repeat this mistake.

IV. WHY DO WE RECOMMEND AGAINST THE NOVA OR C-8 MODE?

It should be clearly understood that our recommendation against the Nova or C-8 Mode at this time refers solely to its use as a launch vehicle for the implementation of the President's commitment to put a man on the moon in this decade. We at Marshall feel very strongly that the Advanced Saturn C-5 is not the end of the line as far as major launch vehicles are concerned! Undoubtedly, as we shall be going about setting up a base on the moon and beginning with the manned exploration of the planets, there will be a great need for launch vehicles more powerful than the C-5. But for these purposes such a new vehicle could be conceived and developed on a more relaxed time schedule. It would be a true follow-on launch vehicle. All of our studies aimed at NASA's needs for a true manned interplanetary capability indicate that a launch vehicle substantially more powerful than one powered by eight F-1 engines would be required. Our recommendation, therefore, should be formulated as follows: "Let us take Nova or C-8 out of the race of putting an American on the moon in this decade, but let us develop a sound concept for a follow-on 'Supernova' launch vehicle".

Here are our reasons for recommending to take Nova or C-8 out of the present Manned Lunar Landing Program:

a. As previously stated, the Apollo system in its present form is not landable on the moon. The spacecraft system would require substantial changes from the presently conceived configuration. The same argument is, of course, applicable to the Earth Orbit Rendezvous Mode.

b. With the S-II stage of the Advanced Saturn C-5 serving as a second stage of a C-8 (boosted by eight F-1 engines) we would have an undesirable, poorly staged, hybrid launch vehicle, with a payload capability far below the maximum obtainable with the same first stage. Performance-wise, with its escape capability of only 132,000 lbs. (in lieu of the 150,000 lbs. demanded) it would still be too marginal, without a high energy return propulsion system, to land the present Apollo Command Module on the surface of the moon.

c. Implementation of the Nova or C-8 program in addition to the Advanced Saturn C-5 would lead to two grossly underfunded and under-managed programs with resulting abject failure of both. Implementation of the Nova or C-8 program in lieu of the Advanced Saturn C-5 would have an absolutely disastrous impact on all our facility plans.

The rafter height of the Michoud plant is 40 feet. The diameter of the S-IC is 33 feet. As a result, most of the assembly operations for the S-IC booster of the C-5 can take place in a horizontal position. Only a relatively narrow high bay tower must be added to the main building for a few operations which must be carried out in a vertical position. A Nova or C-8 booster, however, has a diameter of approximately 50 feet. This means that the roof of a very substantial portion of the Michoud plant would have to be raised by 15 to 20 feet. Another alternative would be to build a very large high bay area where every operation involving cumbersome parts would be done in a vertical position. In either case the very serious question arises whether under these circumstances the Michoud plant was a good selection to begin with.

The foundation situation at Michoud is so poor that extensive pile driving is necessary. This did not bother us when we acquired the plant because the many thousands of piles on which it rests were driven twenty years ago by somebody else. But if we had to enter into a major pile driving operation now, the question would immediately arise as to whether we could not find other building sites where foundations could be prepared cheaper and faster.

Any tampering with the NASA commitment to utilize the Michoud plant, however, would also affect Chrysler's S-1 program, for which tooling and plant preparation are already in full swing at Michoud. Raising the roof and driving thousands of piles in Michoud may turn out to be impossible while Chrysler is assembling S-I's in the same hangar.

In summary, the impact of a switch from C-5 to Nova/C-8 on the very concept of Michoud, would call for a careful and detailed study whose outcome with respect to continued desirability of the use of the Michoud plant appears quite doubtful. We consider it most likely that discontinuance of the C-5 plan in favor of Nova or C-8 would reopen the entire Michoud decision and would throw the entire program into turmoil with ensuing unpredictable delays. The construction of a new plant would take at least 2-1/2 years to beneficial occupancy and over 3 years to start of production.

d. At the Marshall Space Flight Center, construction of a static test stand for S-IC booster is well under way. In its present form this test stand cannot be used for the first stage of Nova or C-8. Studies indicate that as far as the noise level is concerned, there will probably be no objection to firing up eight F-1 engines at MSFC. However, the Marshall test stand construction program would be greatly delayed, regardless of what approach we would take to accommodate Nova/C-8 stages. Detailed studies seem to indicate that the fastest course of action, if Nova or C-8 were adopted, would be to build

- a brand new eight F-1 booster test stand south of the present S-IC test stand, and

- convert the present S-IC test stand into an N-II test stand. (This latter conclusion is arrived at because the firing of an N-II stage at Santa Susanna is not possible for safety reasons, the S-II propellant load being considered the absolute maximum permissible.)

The Mississippi Test Facility is still a "cow pasture that NASA doesn't even own yet", and cannot compete with any test stand availability dates in Huntsville. Developments of basic utilities (roads, water, power, sewage, canals, rail spur, etc.) at MTF will require well over a year, and all scheduling studies indicate that whatever we build at MTF is about 18 months behind comparable facilities built in Huntsville. MTF should, therefore, be considered an acceptance firing and product improvement site for Michoud products rather than a basic development site.

e. In view of the fact that the S-II stage is not powerful enough for the Apollo direct flight mission profile, a second stage powered by eight or nine J-2's or two M-1's is needed. Such a stage would again be on the order of 40 to 50 feet in diameter. No studies have been made as to whether it could be built in the Downey/Seal Beach complex. It is certain, however, that its static testing in Santa Susanna is impossible. As a result, we would have to take an entirely new look at the NAA contract.

f. I have already mentioned the disruptive effect a cancellation of the C-5 would have on the RIFT program.

g. One of the strongest arguments against replacement of the Advanced Saturn C-5 by Nova or C-8 is that such a decision would topple our entire contractor structure. It should be remembered that the temporary uncertainty about the relatively minor question of whether NAA should assemble at Seal Beach or Eglin cost us a delay of almost half a year. I think it should not take much imagination to realize what would happen if we were to tell Boeing, NAA and Douglas that the C-5 was out; that we are going to build a booster with eight F-1 engines, a second stage with eight or nine J-2's or maybe two M-1 engines; and that the entire problem of manufacturing and testing facilities must be re-evaluated.

We already have several thousands of men actually at work on these three stages and many of them have been dislocated from their home plants in implementation of our present C-5 program. Rather than leaving these thousands of men suspended (although supported by NASA dollars) in a state of uncertainty over an extended period of new systems analysis, program implementation studies, budget reshuffles, site selection procedures, etc., it may indeed turn out to be wiser to just terminate the existing contracts and advise the contractors that we will call them back once we have a new program plan laid out for them. We have no doubt that the termination costs incurring to NASA by doing this would easily amount to several hundred million dollars.

I have asked a selected group of key Marshall executives for their appraisal, in terms of delay of the first orbital launch, if the C-5 was to be discontinued and replaced by a Nova or C-8. The estimates of these men (whose duties it would be to implement the new program) varied between 14 and 24 months with an _average_ estimate of an over-all delay of _19 months_.

h. In appraising the total loss to NASA, it should also not be overlooked that we are supporting engine development teams at various contractor plants at the rate of many tens of millions of dollars per year for every stage of C-1 and C-5. If the exact definition of the stages were delayed by switching to Nova/C-8, these engine development teams would have to be held on the NASA payroll for just that much longer, in order to assure proper engine/stage integration.

i. More than twelve months of past extensive effort at the Marshall Space Flight Center to analyze and define the Advanced Saturn C-5 system in a great deal of engineering detail would have to be written off as a flat loss, if we abandoned the C-5 now. This item alone, aside from the time irretrievably lost, represents an expenditure of over one hundred million dollars.

j. The unavoidable uncertainty in many areas created by a switch to Nova or C-8 (Can we retain present C-5 contractors? Where are the new fabrication sites? Where are we going to static test? etc.) may easily lead to delays even well in excess of the estimates given above. For in view of the political pressures invariably exerted on NASA in connection with facility siting decisions, it is quite likely that even the NASA Administrator himself will find himself frequently unable to make binding decisions without demandin from OMSF an extensive re-appraisal of a multitude of issues related with siting. There was ample evidence of this during the past year.

k. For all the reasons quoted above, the Marshall Space Flight Cent considers a discontinuation of the Advanced Saturn C-5 in favor of Nova or C- as the _worst_ of the four proposed modes for implementation of the manned lun landing project. We at Marshall would consider a decision in favor of this mo to be tantamount with giving up the race to put a man on the moon in this deca

IN SUMMARY I THEREFORE RECOMMEND THAT:

a. The Lunar Orbit Rendezvous Mode be adopted.

b. A development of an unmanned, fully automatic, one-way C-5 Logistics Vehicle be undertaken in support of the lunar expedition.

c. The C-1 program as established today be retained and that, in accordance with progress made in S-IVB development, the C-1 be gradually replaced by the C-1B.

d. A C-1B program be officially established and approved with adequate funding.

e. The development of high energy propulsion systems be initiated as a back-up for the Service Module and possibly the Lunar Excursion Module.

f. Supplements to present development contracts to Rocketdyne on the F-1 and J-2 engines be let to increase thrust and/or specific impulse.

Wernher von Braun, Director
George C. Marshall Space Flight Center

George E. Mueller to Director, Manned Spacecraft Center, et al., "Revised Manned Space Flight Schedule," 31 October 1963, "All-Up" Decision File, NASA Historical Reference Collection, NASA Headquarters, Washington, D.C.

In the fall of 1963, as this document shows, the Deputy Associate Administrator for Manned Space Flight made a decision to drop the traditional step-by-step flight tests of rockets and spacecraft components in the interest of speeding the development process. Instead, George Mueller told NASA engineers to assemble all the stages of the Saturn V rocket along with the command and service module and conduct just two or three non-piloted test flights of the whole system. This decision became known as the "All-Up" test procedure. It accelerated the program by at least several months, paying off on 9 November 1967 when NASA successfully launched an "all-up" Saturn/Apollo vehicle.

IN REPLY REFER TO:
M-C M 9330.186

OCT ? · ·???
Oct 31, 1963

TO: Director, Manned Spacecraft Center
Houston 1, Texas

Director, Launch Operations Center
Cocoa Beach, Florida

Director, Marshall Space Flight Center
Huntsville, Alabama

FROM: Deputy Associate Administrator for Manned
Space Flight

SUBJECT: Revised Manned Space Flight Schedule

Recent schedule and budget reviews have resulted in a
deletion of the Saturn I manned flight program and
realignment of schedules and flight mission assignments
on the Saturn IB and Saturn V programs. It is my desire
at this time to plan a flight schedule which has a good
probability of being met or exceeded. Accordingly, I
am proposing that a flight schedule such as shown in
Figure 1, with slight adjustments as required to prevent
"stack-up", be accepted as the official launch schedule.
Contractor schedules for spacecraft and launch vehicle
deliveries should be as shown in Figure 2. This would
allow actual flights to take place several months earlier
than the official schedule. The period after checkout
at the Cape and prior to the official launch date should
be designated the "Space Vehicle Acceptance" period.

With regard to flight missions for Saturn I, MSC should
indicate when they will be in a position to propose a
firm mission and spacecraft configuration for SA-10.
MSFC should indicate the cost of a meteoroid payload
for that flight. SA-6 through SA-9 missions should
remain as presently defined.

CLASSIFICATION CHANGED

To _Unclassified_

Authority of _MSF Sec. Clark office_

Date _4-21-7_ _L. Limmio_

It is my desire that "all-up" spacecraft and launch vehicle flights be made as early as possible in the program. To this end, SA-201 and 501 should utilize all live stages and should carry complete spacecraft for their respective missions. SA-501 and 502 missions should be reentry tests of the spacecraft at lunar return velocity. It is recognized that the Saturn IB flights will have CM/SM and CM/SM/LEM configurations.

Mission planning should consider that two successful flights would be made prior to a manned flight. Thus, 203 could conceivably be the first manned Apollo flight. However, the official schedule would show the first manned flight as 207, with flights 203-206 designated as "man-rating" flights. A similar philosophy would apply to Saturn V for "man-rating" flights with 507 shown as the first manned flight.

I would like your assessment of the proposed schedule, including any effect on resource requirements in FY 1964, 1965 and run-out by November 11, 1963. My goal is to have an official schedule reflecting the philosophy outlined here by November 25, 1963.

George M. Low

George E. Mueller
Deputy Associate Administrator
for Manned Space Flight

Enclosures:
   Figure 1
   Figure 2

TABLE 1 - FLIGHT SCHEDULE

Saturn I

SA-5	Veh. Dev.	Dec. 1963
SA-6	Apollo B/P	Apr. 1964
SA-7	Apollo B/P	Aug. 1964
SA-9	Meteoroid	Dec. 1964
SA-8	Meteoroid	Apr. 1965
SA-10	Undetermined	Aug. 1965

Saturn IB

SA-201	CM/SM		Jan. 1966
SA-202	CM/SM		Apr. 1966
SA-203	CM/SM/LEM		Jul. 1966
SA-204	"	"	Oct. 1966
SA-205	"	"	Dec. 1966
SA-206	"	"	Feb. 1967
SA-207	Manned		Apr. 1967
SA-208	"	"	Jun. 1967
SA-209	"	"	Aug. 1967
SA-210	"	"	Oct. 1967
SA-211	"	"	Dec. 1967
SA-212	"	"	Feb. 1968

Saturn V

SA-501	"All-Up" Vehicle and S/C Reentry		Jan. 1967
SA-502	"	"	Apr. 1967
SA-503	Lunar Mission Conf.		Jul. 1967
SA-504	"	"	Oct. 1967
SA-505	"	"	Dec. 1967
SA-506	"	"	Feb. 1968
SA-507	Manned		Apr. 1968
SA-508	"	"	Jun. 1968
SA-509	"	"	Aug. 1968
SA-510	"	"	Oct. 1968
SA-511	"	"	Dec. 1968
SA-512	"	"	Feb. 1969
SA-513	"	"	Apr. 1969
SA-514	"	"	Jun. 1969
SA-515	"	"	Aug. 1969

FIGURE 2 — DELIVERY SCHEDULE (...)

Present Allowable Delivery Date

SAMPLE X	VEHICLE	A/C
SA-5	Delivered	Delivered
SA-6	Jan. 1964	Jan. 1964
SA-7	May 1964	May 1964
SA-9	Sep. 1964	Sep. 1964
SA-8	Dec. 1964	Dec. 1964
SA-10	Feb. 1965	Undetermined

SATURN I		
SA-201	Aug. 1965	Jun. 1965
SA-202	Nov. 1965	Sep. 1965
SA-203	Feb. 1966	Jan. 1966
SA-204	May 1966	Mar. 1966
SA-205	Jul. 1966	May 1966
SA-206	Sep. 1966	Jul. 1966
SA-207	Nov. 1966	Sep. 1966
SA-208	Jan. 1967	Nov. 1966
SA-209	Mar. 1967	Jan. 1967
SA-210	May 1967	Mar. 1967
SA-211	Jul. 1967	May 1967
SA-212	Sep. 1967	Jul. 1967

SATURN V		
SA-501	Jun. 1966	May 1966
SA-502	Oct. 1966	Aug. 1966
SA-503	Jan. 1967	Nov. 1966
SA-504	Apr. 1967	Feb. 1967
SA-505	Jun. 1967	May 1967
SA-506	Aug. 1967	Jun. 1967
SA-507	Oct. 1967	Aug. 1967
SA-508	Dec. 1967	Oct. 1967
SA-509	Feb. 1968	Dec. 1967
SA-510	Apr. 1968	Feb. 1968
SA-511	Jun. 1968	Apr. 1968
SA-512	Aug. 1968	Jun. 1968
SA-513	Oct. 1968	Aug. 1968
SA-514	Dec. 1968	Oct. 1968
SA-515	Feb. 1969	Dec. 1968

"Report of Apollo 204 Review Board to the Administrator, National Aeronautics and Space Administration," 5 April 1967, Apollo Files, NASA Historical Reference Collection, NASA Headquarters, Washington, D.C.

On 27 January 1967 a fire engulfed the Apollo 204 capsule and killed three astronauts—Gus Grissom, Roger Chaffee, and Edward White. Immediately thereafter NASA Administrator James E. Webb appointed Floyd L. Thompson, director of the Langley Research Center, as the head of an investigative committee. Its report was issued on 5 April 1967, the transmittal letter and findings of which are printed here.

NATIONAL AERONAUTICS AND SPACE ADMINISTRATION

APOLLO 204 REVIEW BOARD

April 5, 1967

The Honorable James E. Webb
Administrator
National Aeronautics and Space Administration
Washington, D. C. 20546

Dear Mr. Webb:

Pursuant to your directive as implemented by the memorandum of
February 3, 1967, signed by the Deputy Administrator, Dr. Robert C.
Seamans, Jr., the Apollo 204 Review Board herewith transmits its
final, formal report, each member concurring in each of the findings,
determinations, and recommendations.

Sincerely,

Dr. Floyd L. Thompson
Chairman

Frank Borman, Col., USAF

Dr. Robert W. Van Dolah

Dr. Maxime A. Faget

George C. White, Jr.

E. Barton Geer

John J. Williams

Charles F. Strang, Col., USAF

Part VI

BOARD FINDINGS, DETERMINATIONS AND RECOMMENDATIONS

In this Review, the Board adhered to the principle that reliability of the Command Module and the entire system involved in its operation is a requirement common to both safety and mission success. Once the Command Module has left the earth's environment the occupants are totally dependent upon it for their safety. It follows that protection from fire as a hazard involves much more than quick egress. The latter has merit only during test periods on earth when the Command Module is being readied for its mission and not during the mission itself. The risk of fire must be faced; however, that risk is only one factor pertaining to the reliability of the Command Module that must received adequate consideration. Design features and operating procedures that are intended to reduce the fire risk must not introduce other serious risks to mission success and safety.

1. FINDING:

    a. There was a momentary power failure at 23:30:55 GMT.

    b. Evidence of several arcs was found in the post fire investigation.

    c. No single ignition source of the fire was conclusively identified.

DETERMINATION:

The most probable initiator was an electrical arc in the sector between the -Y and +Z spacecraft axes. The exact location best fitting the total available information is near the floor in the lower forward section of the left-hand equipment bay where Environmental Control System (ECS) instrumentation power wiring leads into the area between the Environmental Control Unit (ECU) and the oxygen panel. No evidence was discovered that suggested sabotage.

2. FINDING:

    a. The Command Module contained many types and classes of combustible material in areas contiguous to possible ignition sources.

    b. The test was conducted with a 16.7 pounds per square inch absolute, 100 percent oxygen atmosphere.

DETERMINATION:

The test conditions were extremely hazardous.

RECOMMENDATION:

The amount and location of combustible materials in the Command Module must be severely restricted and controlled.

3. FINDING:

    a. The rapid spread of fire caused an increase in pressure and temperature which resulted in rupture of the Command Module and creation of a toxic atmosphere. Death of the crew was from asphyxia due to inhalation of toxic gases due to fire. A contributory cause of death was thermal burns.

    b. Non-uniform distribution of carboxyhemoglobin was found by autopsy.

DETERMINATION:

Autopsy data leads to the medical opinion that unconsciousness occurred rapidly and that death followed soon thereafter.

4. FINDING:

Due to internal pressure, the Command Module inner hatch could not be opened prior to rupture of the Command Module.

DETERMINATION:

The crew was never capable of effecting emergency egress because of the pressurization before rupture and their loss of consciousness soon after rupture.

RECOMMENDATION:

The time required for egress of the crew be reduced and the operations necessary for egress be simplified.

5. FINDING:

Those organizations responsible for the planning, conduct and safety of this test failed to identify it as being hazardous. Contingency preparations to permit escape or rescue of the crew from an internal Command Module fire were not made.

    a. No procedures for this type of emergency had been established either for the crew or for the spacecraft pad work team.

    b. The emergency equipment located in the White Room and on the spacecraft work levels was not designed for the smoke condition resulting from a fire of this nature.

c. Emergency fire, rescue and medical teams were not in attendance.

d. Both the spacecraft work levels and the umbilical tower access arm contain features such as steps, sliding doors and sharp turns in the egress paths which hinder emergency operations.

DETERMINATION:

Adequate safety precautions were neither established nor observed for this test.

RECOMMENDATIONS:

a. Management continually monitor the safety of all test operations and assure the adequacy of emergency procedures.

b. All emergency equipment (breathing apparatus, protective clothing, deluge systems, access arm, etc.) be reviewed for adequacy

c. Personnel training and practice for emergency procedures be given on a regular basis and reviewed prior to the conduct of a hazardous operation.

d. Service structures and umbilical towers be modified to facilitate emergency operations.

6. FINDING:

Frequent interruptions and failures had been experienced in the overall communication system during the operations preceding the accident.

DETERMINATION:

The overall communication system was unsatisfactory.

RECOMMENDATIONS:

a. The Ground Communication System be improved to assure reliable communications between all test elements as soon as possible and before the next manned flight.

b. A detailed design review be conducted on the entire spacecraft communication system.

7. FINDING:

a. Revisions to the Operational Checkout Procedure for the test were issued at 5:30 pm EST January 26, 1967 (209 pages) and 10:00 am EST January 27, 1967 (4 pages).

b. Differences existed between the Ground Test Procedures and the In-Flight Check Lists

DETERMINATION:

Neither the revision nor the differences contributed to the accident. The late issuance of the revision, however, prevented test personnel from becoming adequately familiar with the test procedure prior to its use.

RECOMMENDATIONS:

a. Test Procedures and Pilot's Checklists that represent the actual Command Module configuration be published in final form and reviewed early enough to permit adequate preparation and participation of all test organization .

b. Timely distribution of test procedures and major changes be made a constraint to the beginning of any test.

8. FINDING:

The fire in Command Module 012 was subsequently simulated closely by a test fire in a full-scale mock-up.

DETERMINATION:

Full-scale mock-up fire tests can be used to give a realistic appraisal of fire risks in flight-configured spacecraft.

RECOMMENDATION:

Full-scale mock-ups in flight configuration be tested to determine the risk of fire.

9. FINDING:

The Command Module Environmental Control System design provides a pure oxygen atmosphere.

DETERMINATION:

This atmosphere presents severe fire hazards if the amount and location of combustibles in the Command Module are not restricted and controlled.

RECOMMENDATIONS:

a. The fire safety of the reconfigured Command Module be established by full-scale mock-up tests.

b. Studies of the use of a diluent gas be continued with particular reference to assessing the problems of gas detection and control and the risk of additional operations that would be required in the use of a two gas atmosphere.

10. FINDING:

Deficiencies existed in Command Module design, workmanship and quality control, such as:

a. Components of the Environmental Control System installed in Command Module 012 had a history of many removals and of technical difficulties including regulator failures, line failures and Environmental Control Unit failures. The design and installation features of the Environmental Control Unit makes removal or repair difficult.

b. Coolant leakage at solder joints has been a chronic problem.

c. The coolant is both corrosive and combustible.

d. Deficiencies in design, manufacture, installation, rework and quality control existed in the electrical wiring.

e. No vibration test was made of a complete flight-configured spacecraft.

f. Spacecraft design and operating procedures currently require the disconnecting of electrical connections while powered.

g. No design features for fire protection were incorporated.

DETERMINATION:

These deficiencies created an unnecessarily hazardous condition and their continuation would imperil any future Apollo operations.

RECOMMENDATIONS:

a. An in-depth review of all elements, components and assemblies of the Environmental Control System be conducted to assure its functional and structural integrity and to minimize its contribution to fire risk.

b. Present design of soldered joints in plumbing be modified to increase integrity or the joints be replaced with a more structurally reliable configuration.

c. Deleterious effects of coolant leakage and spillage be eliminated.

d. Review of specifications be conducted, 3-dimensional jigs be used in manufacture of wire bundles and rigid inspection at all stages of wiring design, manufacture and installation be enforced.

e. Vibration tests be conducted of a flight-configured spacecraft.

f. The necessity for electrical connections or disconnections with power on within the crew compartment be eliminated.

g. Investigation be made of the most effective means of controlling and extinguishing a spacecraft fire. Auxiliary breathing oxygen and crew protection from smoke and toxic fumes be provided.

11. FINDING:

An examination of operating practices showed the following examples of problem areas:

a. The number of the open items at the time of shipment of the Command Module 012 was not known. There were 113 significant Engineering Orders not accomplished at the time Command Module 012 was delivered to NASA; 623 Engineering Orders were released subsequent to delivery. Of these, 22 were recent releases which were not recorded in configuration records at the time of the accident.

b. Established requirements were not followed with regard to the pre-test constraints list. The list was not completed and signed by designated contractor and NASA personnel prior to the test, even though oral agreement to proceed was reached.

c. Formulation of and changes to pre-launch test requirements for the Apollo spacecraft program were unresponsive to changing conditions.

d. Non-certified equipment items were installed in the Command Module at time of test.

e. Discrepancies existed between NAA and NASA MSC specifications regarding inclusion and positioning of flammable materials.

f. The test specification was released in August 1966 and was not updated to include accumulated changes from release date to date of the test.

DETERMINATION:

Problems of program management and relationships between Centers and with the contractor have led in some cases to insufficient response to changing program requirements.

RECOMMENDATION:

Every effort must be made to insure the maximum clarification and understanding of the responsibilities of all the organizations involved, the objective being a fully coordinated and efficient program.

NASA Apollo Program Director, to NASA Associate Administrator for Manned Space Flight, "Apollo 8 Mission Selection," 11 November 1968, Apollo 8 Files, NASA Historical Reference Collection, NASA Headquarters, Washington, D.C.

In the aftermath of the tragic Apollo 204 capsule fire in 1967, NASA's goal of reaching the Moon before the end of the decade seemed in jeopardy. It took almost twenty months after the fire, until October 1968, before astronauts were launched into orbit aboard an Apollo spacecraft. The success of this test flight, however, prompted the Apollo program manager, Air Force General Samuel C. Phillips, to suggest a bold strategy for regaining momentum in the lunar landing program. He recommended in November 1968 that the next Apollo flight be recast as a circumlunar mission. His memorandum, accepted by the NASA administrator on 18 November 1968, made possible the dramatic mission of *Apollo 8* on 21-27 December 1968.

UNITED STATES GOVERNMENT

Memorandum

TO : M/Associate Administrator for Manned Space Flight DATE: 11 NOV 1968

FROM : MA/Apollo Program Director

SUBJECT: Apollo 8 Mission Selection

The purpose of this memorandum is to obtain your approval to fly Apollo 8 on an open-ended lunar orbit mission in December 1968.

My recommendation is based on an exhaustive review of pertinent technical and operational factors and also on careful consideration of the impact that either a success or a failure in this mission will have on our ability to carry out the manned lunar landing in 1969.

THE APOLLO 8 C' LUNAR ORBIT MISSION:

Attachment I to this memorandum contains a detailed description of the Apollo 8 lunar orbit mission. Significant features of this mission plan are:

Planned Schedule:

Launch: 0750 EST, 21 December 1968
Translunar Injection: 1040 EST, 21 December 1968
Lunar Orbit Insertion:
    LOI$_1$ Initiate: (60X170 NM Orbit) 0457 EST, 24 December 1968
    LOI$_2$ Initiate: (60 NM Circular Orbit) 0921 EST, 24 December 1968
Transearth Injection: 0105 EST, 25 December 1968
Landing: 1053 EST, 27 December 1968

Alternate Schedule:

Monthly Launch Windows: 21-27 December 1968 or as soon thereafter
                        as possible.
Daily Launch Windows: Approximately 5 hours duration.

Open-Ended Mission Concept:

A large number of abort and alternate mission options are provided for in the Mission Plan and associated Mission Rules. Noteworthy examples of the way in which this open-ended concept could operate in this mission are the following:

    A low earth orbital mission in the event of a "no go" in earth orbit prior to translunar injection.

Early return to earth in event of certain malfunction conditions during translunar coast.

A circumlunar mission in event of a "no go" during checkout prior to the lunar orbit insertion burn.

APOLLO 8 MISSION SELECTION:

On August 19, 1968, we announced the decision to fly Apollo 8 as a Saturn V, CSM-only mission. The basic plan provided for Apollo 8 to fly a low earth orbital mission, but forward alternatives were to be considered up to and including a lunar orbital mission. Final decision was to be reserved pending completion of the Apollo 7 mission and a series of detailed reviews of all elements of the Apollo 8 mission including the space vehicle, launch complex, operational support system, and mission planning.

Apollo 7 Mission Results:

An important factor in the total decision process leading to my recommendation has been and continues to be the demonstrated performance of the Apollo 7 Command and Service Module (CSM) subsystems, and the compatibility of the CSM with crew functions, and the Manned Space Flight Network. Comprehensive understanding of all Apollo 7 flight anomalies and their impact on a lunar mission is fundamental to arriving at a proper decision. Attachment II to this memorandum provides a recap of the Apollo 7 flight anomalies, their disposition, and a statement of any known risk remaining on the proposed Apollo 8 mission together with the actions proposed.

Apollo 4 and Apollo 6 Results:

The results of the Apollo 4 and Apollo 6 missions, in which the performance of the 501 and 502 Saturn V launch vehicles was tested, have been carefully analyzed. All flight anomalies have been resolved. In particular, the two most significant problems encountered in Apollo 6--longitudinal oscillation or "POGO" effect in the first stage of the Saturn V and the rupture of small propellant lines in the upper stages--have been corrected and the solutions verified in extensive ground tests.

Meetings and Reviews:

The decision process, resulting in my recommendation, has included a comprehensive series of reviews conducted over the past several weeks to examine in detail all facets of the considerations involved in planning for and providing a capability to fly Apollo 8 on a lunar orbit mission. The calendar for and purpose of these meetings are presented in Attachment III. An important milestone was achieved with successful completion of the Design Certification Review on November 7, 1968. A copy of the signed Design Certification is appended as Attachment IV.

Pros and Cons of a Lunar Orbital Flight:

My objective through this period has been to bring into meaningful perspective the trade-offs between total program risk and gain resulting from introduction of a CSM-only lunar orbit mission on Apollo 8 into the total mission sequence leading to the earliest possible successful Apollo lunar landing and return. As you know, this assessment process is inherently judgmental in nature. Many factors have been considered, the evaluation of which supports a recommendation to proceed forward with an Apollo 8 open-ended lunar orbit mission. These factors are:

PROS:

Mission Readiness:

- The CSM has been designed and developed to perform a lunar orbit mission and has performed very well on four unmanned and one manned flights (CSM's 009, 011, 017, 020, and 101).

- We have learned all that we need in earth orbital operation except repetition of performance already demonstrated.

- The extensive qualification and endurance-type sub-system ground testing conducted over the past 18 months on the CSM equipments has contributed to a high level of system maturity, as demonstrated by the Apollo 7 flight.

- Performance of Apollo 7 systems has been thoroughly reviewed, and no indication has been evidenced of design deficiency.

- Detailed analysis of Apollo 4 and Apollo 6 launch vehicle anomalies, followed by design modifications and rigorous ground testing gives us high confidence in successful performance of the Apollo 8 launch vehicle.

- By design all subsystems affecting crew survival (Environmental Control System, Electrical Power System, Reaction Control System, and Guidance and Navigation System) are redundant and can suffer significant degradation without crew or mission loss. The sole exceptions are the injector and thrust chamber of the Service Propulsion System. These two engine components are of simple, rugged design, with high structural and thermal safety margins. (See Attachment V.)

. Excellent consumables and performance margins exist for the first CSM lunar mission because of the reduction in performance requirements represented by omitting the weight of the lunar module. An example of the predicted spacecraft consumables usage is provided below to illustrate this point:

Consumable	Total Usable	Total Used	Reserve
Service Module Reaction Control System Propellant (Pounds)	1140	294.5	845.5
Command Module Reaction Control System Propellant (Pounds)	231.2	29.4	201.8
Service Propulsion System Propellant (Pounds)	40,013	28,987	11,026
Cryogenic Oxygen (Pounds)	640	410	230
Cryogenic Hydrogen (Pounds)	56	40	16

PROS:

Effect on Program Progress:

The lunar orbit mission will:

. Provide valuable operational experience on a lunar CSM mission for flight and ground and recovery crews. This will enhance probability of success on the subsequent more complex lunar missions by permitting training emphasis on phases of these missions as yet untried.

. Provide an opportunity to evaluate the quality of MSFN and on-board navigation in lunar orbit including the effects of local orbit perturbations. This will increase anticipated accuracy of rendezvous maneuvers and lunar touchdown on a lunar landing mission.

. Permit validation of Apollo CSM communications and navigation systems at lunar distance.

. Serve to improve consumables requirements prediction
techniques.

. Complete the final verification of the ground support
elements and the onboard computer programs.

. Increase the depth of understanding of thermal conditions in deep space and lunar proximity.

. Confirm the astronauts' ability to see, use, and photograph landmarks during a lunar mission.

. Provide an early opportunity for additional photographs
for operational and scientific uses such as augmenting
Lunar Orbiter coverage and for obtaining data for training
crewmen on terrain identification under different lighting
conditions.

CONS:

Mission Readiness:

. Marginal design conditions in the Block II CSM may not
have been uncovered with only one manned flight.

. The life of the crew depends on the successful operation
of the Service Propulsion System during the Transearth
Injection maneuver.

. The three days endurance level required of backup systems
in the event of an abort from a lunar orbit mission is greate
than from an earth orbit mission.

CONS:

Effect on Program Progress:

. Validation of Colossus spacecraft software program and
Real Time Computer Complex ground software program could
be accomplished in a high earth orbital mission.

. Only landmark sightings and lunar navigation require a
lunar mission to validate.

Impact of Success or Failure on Accomplishing Lunar Landing in 1969:

A successful mission will:

. Represent a significant new international achievement in space.

- Offer flexibility to capitalize on success and advance the progress of the total program towards a lunar landing without unreasonable risk.

- Provide a significant boost to the morale of the entire Apollo program, and an impetus which must, inevitably enhance our probability of successful lunar landing in 1969.

A mission failure will:

- Delay ultimate accomplishment of the lunar landing mission.

- Provide program critics an opportunity to denounce the Apollo 8 mission as precipitous and unconservative.

RECOMMENDATION:

In conclusion, but with the proviso that all open work against the Apollo 8 open-ended lunar orbit mission is completed and certified, I request your approval to proceed with the implementation plan required to support an earliest December 21, 1968, launch readiness date.

Sam C. Phillips
Lt. General, USAF

Attachments

NASA, Manned Spacecraft Center, "Apollo 11 Technical Air-to-Ground Voice transcription," July 1969, pp. 317-19, 375-77, Apollo 11 Files, NASA Historical Reference Collection, NASA Headquarters, Washington, D.C.

After eight years of all-out effort, nearly $20 billion expended, and three astronauts' deaths, on 20 July 1969 *Apollo 11* landed on the Moon. The two astronauts who set foot on the surface, Neil A. Armstrong and Edwin E. Aldrin, called it in what later astronauts thought of as an understatement, "magnificent desolation." This document contains the radio transmissions of the landing and Armstrong's first venture out onto the Lunar surface. The "CC" in the transcript is Houston Mission Control, CDR is Neil Armstrong, and LMP is Buzz Aldrin.

04 06 45 52	LMP (EAGLE)	413 is in.
04 06 45 57	CC	We copy you down, Eagle.
04 06 45 59	CDR (TRANQ)	Houston, Tranquility Base here.
04 06 46 04	CDR (TRANQ)	THE EAGLE HAS LANDED.
04 06 46 06	CC	Roger, Tranquility. We copy you on the ground. You got a bunch of guys about to turn blue. We're breathing again. Thanks a lot.
04 06 46 16	CDR (TRANQ)	Thank you.
04 06 46 18	CC	You're looking good here.
04 06 46 23	CDR (TRANQ)	Okay. We're going to be busy for a minute.
04 06 46 25	LMP (TRANQ)	MASTER ARM, ON. Take care of the ... I'll get this ...
04 06 46 38	LMP (TRANQ)	Very smooth touchdown.
04 06 46 52	LMP (TRANQ)	...
04 06 47 03	LMP (TRANQ)	Okay. It looks like we're venting the oxidizer now.
04 06 47 06	CC	Roger, Eagle. And you are STAY for - -
04 06 47 08	LMP (TRANQ)	...
04 06 47 09	CC	- - T1. Over. Eagle, you are STAY for T1.
04 06 47 12	CDR (TRANQ)	Roger. Understand, STAY for T1.
04 06 47 15	CC	Roger. And we see you venting the OX.
04 06 47 20	LMP (TRANQ)	Roger.

04 06 47 36	LMP (TRANQ)	... circuit breaker.
04 06 48 10	LMP (TRANQ)	... copy NOUN 60, NOUN 43. Over.
04 06 48 13	CC	Roger. We have it.
04 06 48 14	CMP (COLUMBIA)	Houston, how do you read Columbia on the high gain?
04 06 48 17	CC	Roger - -
04 06 48 18	LMP (TRANQ)	...
04 06 48 19	CC	- - We read you five-by, Columbia. He has landed, Tranquility Base. Eagle is at Tranquility. Over.
04 06 48 26	CMP (COLUMBIA)	Yes. I heard the whole thing.
04 06 48 27	CC	... good show.
04 06 48 31	CMP (COLUMBIA)	Fantastic.
04 06 48 32	LMP (TRANQ)	Engine STOP-RESET.
04 06 48 58	CMP (COLUMBIA)	Houston, Columbia went UPTELEMETRY COMMAND, RESET, to reacquire on the high gain.
04 06 49 02	CC	Copy. Out.
04 06 49 39	CC	Eagle, Houston. You loaded R2 wrong. We want 10254.
04 06 49 50	LMP (TRANQ)	Roger.
04 06 50 28	LMP (TRANQ)	And do you want V horizontal 5515.2?
04 06 50 32	CC	That's affirmative.
04 06 50 59	LMP (TRANQ)	Like - AGS to PGNS align. Over.
04 06 51 04	CC	Say again?

04 06 51 08	LMP (TRANQ)	Like an AGS to PGNS align. Over.
04 06 51 11	CC	Roger. We're standing by for it.
04 06 51 41	LMP (TRANQ)	... quantity ...
04 06 51 45	CC	Eagle, Houston. You are STAY for T2. Over.
04 06 51 50	CC	Correction, you're - -
04 06 51 52	CDR (TRANQ)	Roger. STAY for T2. We thank you.
04 06 51 54	CC	Roger, sir.
04 06 53 37	CC	Tranquility Base, Houston. We recommend you exit P12. Over.
04 06 55 16	CDR (TRANQ)	Hey, Houston, that may have seemed like a very long final phase. The AUTO targeting was taking us right into a football-field size - football-field sized crater, with a large number of big boulders and rocks for about ... one or two crater diameters around it, and it required a ... in P66 and flying manually over the rock field to find a reasonably good area.
04 06 55 49	CC	Roger. We copy. It was beautiful from here, Tranquility. Over.
04 06 56 02	LMP (TRANQ)	We'll get to the details of what's around here, but it looks like a collection of just about every variety of shape, angularity, granularity, about every variety of rock you could find. The colors - Well, it varies pretty much depending on how you're looking relative to the zero-phase point. There doesn't appear to be too much of a general color at all. However, it looks as though some of the rocks and boulders, of which there are quite a few in the near area, it looks as though they're going to have some interesting colors to them. Over.
04 06 56 47	CC	Roger. Copy. Sounds good to us, Tranquility. We'll let you press on through the simulated countdown, and we'll talk to you later. Over.
04 06 57 00	CDR (TRANQ)	Roger.

04 13 18 14	CDR (TRANQ)	That's okay?
04 13 18 15	LMP (TRANQ)	That's good. You've got plenty of room to your left. It's a little close on the ***.
04 13 18 28	CDR (TRANQ)	How am I doing?
04 13 18 29	LMP (TRANQ)	You're doing fine.
04 13 18 51	LMP (TRANQ)	Okay. Do you want those bags?
04 13 18 53	CDR (TRANQ)	Yes. Got it.
04 13 19 16	CDR (TRANQ)	Okay. Houston, I'm on the porch.
04 13 19 20	CC	Roger, Neil.
04 13 19 36	LMP (TRANQ)	Okay. Stand by, Neil.
04 13 19 37	CC	Columbia, Columbia, this is Houston. One minute and 30 seconds to LOS. All systems GO. Over.
04 13 19 46	CMP (COLUMBIA)	Columbia. Thank you.
04 13 19 47	LMP (TRANQ)	Stay where you are a minute, Neil.
04 13 19 48	CDR (TRANQ)	Okay. Need a little slack?
04 13 20 38	CDR (TRANQ)	You need more slack, Buzz?
04 13 20 40	LMP (TRANQ)	No. Hold it just a minute.
04 13 20 41	CDR (TRANQ)	Okay.
04 13 20 56	LMP (TRANQ)	Okay. Everything's nice and straight in here.

*** Three asterisks denote clipping of word and phrases.

| 04 13 20 58 | CDR (TRANQ) | Okay. Can you pull the door open a little more? |

883 on The Coming

04 13 21 00	LMP (TRANQ)	All right.
04 12 21 03	CDR (TRANQ)	Okay.
04 13 21 07	LMP (TRANQ)	Did you get the MESA out?
04 13 21 09	CDR (TRANQ)	I'm going to pull it now.
04 13 21 18	CDR (TRANQ)	Houston, the MESA came down all right.
04 13 21 22	CC	This is Houston. Roger. We copy. And we're standing by for your TV.
04 13 21 39	CDR (TRANQ)	Houston, this is Neil. Radio check.
04 13 21 42	CC	Neil, this is Houston. Loud and clear. Break. Break. Buzz, this is Houston. Radio check, and verify TV circuit breaker in.
04 13 21 54	LMP (TRANQ)	Roger, TV circuit breaker's in, and read you five-square.
04 13 22 00	CC	Roger. We're getting a picture on the TV.
04 13 22 09	LMP (TRANQ)	You got a good picture, huh?
04 13 22 11	CC	There's a great deal of contrast in it, and currently it's upside-down on our monitor, but we can make out a fair amount of detail.
04 13 22 28	LMP (TRANQ)	Okay. Will you verify the position - the opening I ought to have on the camera?
04 13 22 34	CC	Stand by.
04 13 22 48	CC	Okay. Neil, we can see you coming down the ladder now.
04 13 22 59	CDR (TRANQ)	Okay. I just checked getting back up to that first step, Buzz. It's - not even collapsed too far, but it's adequate to get back up.

04 13 23 10	CC	Roger. We copy.
04 13 23 11	CDR (TRANQ)	It takes a pretty good little jump.
04 13 23 25	CC	Buzz, this is Houston. F/2 - 1/160th second for shadow photography on the sequence camera.
04 13 23 35	LMP (TRANQ)	Okay.
04 13 23 38	CDR (TRANQ)	I'm at the foot of the ladder. The LM footpads are only depressed in the surface about 1 or 2 inches, although the surface appears to be very, very fine grained, as you get close to it. It's almost like a powder. Down there, it's very fine.
04 13 23 13	CDR (TRANQ)	I'm going to step off the LM now.
04 13 24 48	CDR (TRANQ)	THAT'S ONE SMALL STEP FOR MAN, ONE GIANT LEAP FOR MANKIND.
04 13 24 48	CDR (TRANQ)	And the - the surface is fine and powdery. I can - I can pick it up loosely with my toe. It does adhere in fine layers like powdered charcoal to the sole and sides of my boots. I only go in a small fraction of an inch, maybe an eighth of an inch, but I can see the footprints of my boots and the treads in the fine, sandy particles.
04 13 25 30	CC	Neil, this is Houston. We're copying.
04 13 25 45	CDR	There seems to be no difficulty in moving around as we suspected. It's even perhaps easier than the simulations at one-sixth g that we performed in the various simulations on the ground. It's actually no trouble to walk around. Okay. The descent engine did not leave a crater of any size. It has about 1 foot clearance on the ground. We're essentially on a very level place here. I can see some evidence of rays emanating from the descent engine, but a very insignificant amount.
04 13 26 54	CDR	Okay, Buzz, we ready to bring down the camera?
04 13 26 59	LMP	I'm all ready. I think it's been all squared away and in good shape.
04 13 27 03	CDR	Okay.

President Richard Nixon to Director, Apollo Program, 21 March 1972, Richard Nixon Files, NASA Historical Reference Collection, NASA Headquarters, Washington, D.C.

At the conclusion of the Apollo program in 1972 Richard Nixon, who had called in 1969 the *Apollo 11* the most significant six days in the history of Earth since the creation, wrote a letter of congratulation to the NASA team that had carried out the Kennedy mandate of landing on the Moon. Rocco Petrone, Apollo Program Director, added his own congratulation to that of the president's in this commemorative document.

NATIONAL AERONAUTICS AND SPACE ADMINISTRATION
WASHINGTON, D C   20546

March 24, 1972

REPLY TO
ATTN OF

Fellow Members of the Apollo Team:

I have received the following letter from President Nixon
in which he said he wanted the Apollo Team to know how much
this nation values the work we have done and are doing in
the Apollo Program. The letter was addressed to me but the
President's words were really addressed to each of you.

I am pleased to pass along the President's words which each
of you has done so much to earn.

Sincerely,

Rocco A. Petrone
Apollo Program Director

THE WHITE HOUSE

WASHINGTON

March 21, 1972

Dear Dr. Petrone:

As we approach the final countdown for Apollo 16, I
want you and all the men and women of Apollo to know
how much this nation values your splendid efforts. The
moon flight program has captured the imagination of
our times as has no other human endeavor. You and
your team have, in fact, written the first chapter in
the history of man's exploration of space, and all
future achievements must credit all of you for having
blazed the path.

Countless people throughout the world will soon be
sharing with you the excitement of Apollo 16's voyage, and I know I speak for all of them in conveying
to you my warmest best wishes for a safe and
successful flight. Good luck!

Sincerely,

Richard Nixon

Dr. Rocco A. Petrone
Director, Apollo Program
Office of Manned Space Flight
National Aeronautics and
   Space Administration
Washington, D. C. 20546

INDEX